Magers and Quinn   **$12.99**

~~~~ \//Bact History\

M000190116

Vilém Flusser

POST-HISTORY

TRANSLATED BY RODRIGO MALTEZ NOVAES

FLUSSER ARCHIVE COLLECTION

EDITED BY SIEGFRIED ZIELINSKI

Pós-História - Vinte instantâneos e um modo de usar
- published by Duas Cidades, 1983 -

Translated from Portuguese by Rodrigo Maltez Novaes
as *Post-History*

First Edition
Minneapolis © 2013, Univocal Publishing

Published by Univocal
123 North 3rd Street, #202
Minneapolis, MN 55401
www.univocalpublishing.com

This book has been published with support from the
Brazilian Ministry of Culture / National Library Foundation.

Obra publicada com o apoio do
Ministério da Cultura do Brasil / Fundação Biblioteca Nacional.

MINISTÉRIO DA CULTURA
Fundação BIBLIOTECA NACIONAL

Thanks to the Vilém Flusser Archive at the Universität der Künste Berlin,
Dinah Flusser, Miguel Flusser, Edith Flusser, Claudia Becker,
Norval Baitello Jr., Michael Boudreaux,
Kenton Card, Meredith Forbes, Tim Syth, and John Ebert.

Designed & Printed by Jason Wagner
Distributed by the University of Minnesota Press

ISBN 9781937561093
Library of Congress Control Number 2012955097

TABLE OF CONTENTS

Flusser Archive Collection

Vilém Flusser is one of the most influential thinkers of media and cultural theory as well as the philosophy of communication in the second half of the 20th century. But unlike certain thinkers of media culture such as Marshall McLuhan or Jean Baudrillard, most of his work has yet to attain the proper attention of the reading public inside and outside the walls of the academy. One of the reasons for this is due to the singular process by which Flusser constructed his thinking and writing. He is a rare polyglot who would write his texts in various languages until he was satisfied with the outcome. Fluent in Czech, German, French, English, and Portuguese, he has left an archive full of thousands of manuscripts in various languages. The Flusser Archive Collection will be a monumental step forward in finally providing an Anglophone readership with a collection of some of Flusser's most important works.

TRANSLATOR'S INTRODUCTION

I do not have free will; I am not free. I am a functionary of programs that are alien to me; I am an instrument. Not being free I do not surprise. I am predictable. History (as a flux of surprising and unpredictable happenings) has been overcome. I function within a post-historical situation, a messianic situation, I am in paradise.

The lack of surprise, the lack of an unprogrammed future is unbearable. Paradise is unbearable. It bores and nauseates me. I must rebel. Can I rebel? I believe I can. The sensation of boredom and nausea that the programs cause in me are experiential proof that I am not completely programmed.

-Vilém Flusser 1966, On Program in *O Diário* newspaper, São Paulo.

Post-History, by Vilém Flusser, focuses on a critique of contemporary values; where they originate and how they are stored and transmitted across generations and throughout the different cultures of the so-called Western world. For this, Flusser explores primarily the concept of "models," because models not only stand for applied values, but also because they are principally of a visual nature – this being the significant aspect that he wants us to note, that values are now inherent in all visual aspects of our culture and therefore embedded in the way that we imagine the world. That values are now of an aesthetic nature should not be underestimated. Politics are now visual (aesthetic), so that one of the principal questions that Flusser raises is, How and when do models change? As well as: Why do they change? The answers are neither simple nor straightforward. But in the opening essay of the book, "The Ground We Tread," he starts by stating that our current situation has become empty of values, in the sense that our progress has become aimless. We no longer know what we are progressing toward and thus have lost our faith in progress.

He draws his primary comparison with the Baroque, when the Counter-Reformation sought to revive Catholic models. And by stating that we are as counter-reformist today as the Baroque, the author suggests that we are also desperately trying to revive old models, since we no longer have a clear view of where our models, and therefore our values, come from today. A sure indicator of the importance of "The Ground We Tread" is that it exists in twelve different versions in four different languages. Flusser constantly reworked his essays through translation, using it as a method to improve the text by being forced to take on the different ontological positions imposed by different languages.

The researcher or translator of Flusser's work is immediately presented with a Borgesian maze of different versions, both published and unpublished, making the pursuit of a true or final version of a work an impossible task. Flusser reworked many of his important titles in different languages. However, he did not do this with everything he wrote; for example, several of his early manuscripts from the 60s extist in only one version, primarily Portuguese. It was mainly during the 70s, the period when he returned to live in Europe, that he actively employed the translation method as a tool for working with his texts. Although he wrote several manuscripts in German and Portuguese during this time, *Post-History* was the first text to which Flusser applied this method. All of the different versions have been consulted for this translation, but only as a guideline and not with the intention of generating a synthesized "final" version, as that would not only be impossible, but pointless.

The initial essays that eventually became the present book were first written as lectures to be delivered at universities in Brazil, France and Israel during the late 1970s. The typescript for this book has four versions: French (partial version), Portuguese (two versions), German (two versions) and English (partial version). The English translation presented here follows the first Portuguese version published in Brazil in 1983 by Duas Cidades in São Paulo, copy edited by Flusser's close friend and correspondent, Milton Vargas.

In each of the essays of *Post-History*, Flusser explores the emergence of a new model, that of the apparatus, and explores its concepts in relation to the work of other thinkers. In a letter to Milton Vargas dated October 22nd, 1980, he lists the title of each essay and includes next to it a list of whom he was arguing for and/or against in each of the texts: "The Ground We Tread" (H. Arendt), "Our Sky" (M. Buber), "Our Program" (R. Carnap), "Our Work" (K. Marx), "Our Knowledge" (K. Popper), "Our Health"

(L. Wittgenstein), "Our Communication" (A. Moles), "Our Rhythm" (H. Marcuse), "Our Dwelling" (J. Ortega y Gasset), "Our Shrinking" (J. Habermas), "Our Clothes" (T. W. Adorno), "Our Images" (M. McLuhan), "Our Game" (A. Rappaport), "Our Diversion" (E. Husserl), "Our Wait" (E. Bloch), "Our Dread" (The Hudson Institute), "Our Inebriation" (M. Heidegger), "Our School" (J. Dewey), "Our Relations" (J. P. Sartre) and "Return" (F. Kafka). And although Flusser deals with the concept of apparatus in many of his previous books, as this was a concept that already preoccupied him since the early 60s, this book became his first full critique of what he saw as a shift in our worldview due to the impact of technical apparatus. In his main argument, Flusser suggests that our times may be characterized by the term "program," much in the same way that the 16th century is loosely characterized by the term "virtue," the 17th by "nature," the 18th by "reason" and the 19th by "progress." And in suggesting this shift in worldview he then provokes by asking: If I function within a predictable programmed reality, can I rebel? And how can I do it? The answer comes swiftly: Only malfunctioning programs and apparatus allow for freedom. Only a malfunctioning functionary can hope for freedom. The essence of freedom is unpredictability. But once co-opted and objectified by apparatus and their programs, all that is left for us is a life of bored contentment within the nauseating technical paradise of a predictable eternal return of the same.

This technical paradise is a post-industrial society, a technocratic society where apparatus produce and maintain a fully automated reality where we no longer have to work, in the sense of imprinting values, or information, onto objects, where we no longer pro-duce. In automation what is significant is that it is not the machines that will become emancipated from man, but that the work performed by them will in turn emancipate man from work so that he may then focus on information production, or in other words on value production. That is the drive behind the desire for technical ecstasy. Being no longer productive, no longer having to deal with objects, the Other then becomes our object, to be hammered and manipulated. Post-industrial society is a "Vampyroteuthian" society, a society of artifice and lies, of surfaces. In this situation, culture becomes the result of automated functions. Full automation is dependent on the application of fixed universal values. And if technical apparatus function according to Boolean algebra, according to binary values, then these are the values they impose onto the world. So that by subjecting ourselves to a world of technical ecstasy, which is the reality of a society of fully automated apparatus systems, a post-industrial, cybernetic society, we would then be not only taking a step back into a world of absolute, dualistic moral values, but also into a world where apparatus could take over the process of decision-making from human intervention, which in fact is already happening. The practice of High Frequency Trading in the large stock exchanges of the world is already a good example of this. Therefore, this technical ecstasy, this technocratic paradise, in Flusser's view, is in fact our hell on Earth. However this dystopian view is not in fact lacking in hope, even if very faint, of the possibility that it will not be realized. A parallel could even be drawn between the dystopian worldview of

Post-History and that of Aldous Huxley's *Brave New World*. The concepts contained in both are not too distant and in fact Flusser was a reader of Huxley's work. But whereas Huxley maintained a continued conviction that his view was in fact correct and would eventually be realized, Flusser on the other hand harbored a subliminal hope that he was perhaps wrong in his prognostications, despite all the indications to the contrary.

Shortly after completing the manuscripts of *Post-History*, he embarked on what became his most eccentric book, *Vampyroteuthis infernalis*, which also had two distinctly different versions in German and Portuguese, focused on an exploration of a new model for humanity, that of a synthesis between human reason and vampyroteuthian love. The period of the late 70s and early 80s was a highly productive phase for the author and some of his most famous titles date from this period. The Vilém Flusser Archive at the Universität der Künste in Berlin, under the Directorship of Siegfried Zielinski, holds all of Flusser's manuscripts and it is possible to estimate that of everything he ever wrote, only thirty percent has been published and mainly in Portuguese and German. The few English translations that have been available up until 2011 are all translated from the German versions of the respective texts, which means that an imbalance was being established that favored only one specific facet of Flusser's work, his German texts. Now with the forthcoming titles in this series, this imbalance will be addressed and eventually the Anglophone world will finally be able to access both facets of the work of this prolific writer.

One other important point to mention is Flusser's particular writing style. The essayistic style that he developed and applied was established during the 60s when he was writing in Brazil and publishing in Brazilian newspapers. During this period he was also giving independent courses at the Brazilian Institute of Philosophy (IBF), the Institute of Technology and Aeronautics (ITA) and the Polytechnic School of the University of São Paulo. All of the courses he delivered were written as short essays to be read out loud to the students and then discussed. Subsequently, all of the courses were compiled as a series and prepared for publishing as books, much in the same way that José Ortega y Gasset prepared his essays for publication as books after being delivered either as lectures or published in periodicals. However, only one course from this period was published in ITA's annual magazine. The other courses were archived and some will be published as part of this series. But the significant point to make in relation to his writing style is that apart from using Ortega y Gasset as a stylistic model, Flusser's style was developed as a result of writing directly for a specific audience, that of students and newspaper readers.

This generated a style that is on the one hand direct, fluid, and radically non-academic. Flusser's texts are essentially Zarathustrian, in the sense that they are for all and none. And on the other hand, his style is also informed by his love of poetry, which is evident above all in the visual style of his work, which has a "metric" all its own. Because of this, when reading Flusser, it might be useful for the reader to have that in mind. What may seem at times idiosyncratic punctuation or phraseology is in fact a very finely considered style that has the specific aim of causing a plastic effect in the reader's mind. This is perhaps one of the most important aspects to keep in mind when translating his texts and one which I take very close to heart. The first thing one notices when reading Flusser's own versions in different languages, is that the visual style is the same, which clearly indicates that this was not accidental or the result of a lack of knowledge of the language in question. Therefore, I tend to resist any attempt to modify or standardize the texts specifically for a contemporary Anglophone reader. His style is just as singular in its Portuguese version, so that the English translations should have, if not the same style, then at least the closest possible.

One of my interpretations of his writing style is that for him the text on the page works very much like a musical score, where each syllable is a note and the punctuation marks the rhythm of the text. The reader may verify this by reading the texts out loud, as in fact Flusser wished them to be read, followed by discussion. These are texts that may be read and studied in private, but which were primarily written to be read in the company of others. And when read to others, the musical quality of his work may then be fully appreciated. The real challenge for the translator is of course to be able to reproduce the same rhythm in English. The challenges posed to the translator are both difficult and rewarding in equal measure. However, one thing is certain; Flusser's style never leaves anyone indifferent to it, the reader's passions are always moved in one direction or another, which is the result of a carefully considered and applied method by the author. Equally singular is his use of terminology, which, it should be noted, is always applied in the strict sense. What may seem at times to be an old fashioned idiomatic style is again a very meticulous use of words according to their past and present meaning, especially in relation to their etymological root and the possibilities it affords for the exploration of concepts using double and sub-textual meanings, perhaps forgotten because of continuously evolving semantic variations and modulations. With this in mind, it is better now to cease with explanatory attempts and to allow you, the reader, to discover Flusser on your own terms.

Rodrigo Maltez Novaes
Berlin, November 2012

POST-HISTORY

User's Manual

The following essays are lectures. They were read at Universities and they all took approximately "fifty academic minutes" in order to be read out loud. That is: their content is dense and demands to be discussed during a subsequent seminar. There is a difference between spoken texts and read ones. Reading may be interrupted and intercalated by thought. The following essays want to be read at leisure or discussed.

These lectures were delivered in Marseilles, Jerusalem and São Paulo. The author hopes that this fact does not make itself evident in the text. Because the text not only seeks to "overcome" *history* but also *geography*. The text wants to be distant precisely because it wants to reach the concrete that hides behind history and geography. That is: although it was delivered at "academies" it wants deliberately to escape academicism. And it is necessary to have this in mind in order for a "correct" reading.

Originally the text was written in French and English without the intention to publish. It was translated to German to be published. The present Portuguese version will be published in Brazil, an environment in which the author is engaged and wishes it to be a contribution to the Brazilian dialogue. It must be read with this in mind.

The sequence of the essays is random: they can be read in any order. Nevertheless there is a discursive thread that orders the essays. This is a discourse that runs from despair toward hope, however tenuous. Whoever follows this course must have read the text in the correct order. Although an equally useful method would be to read the text in leaps, like the movement of the knight on a chessboard. This method will allow the unmasking of the methodical tricks (para-phenomenological), to which the author appealed.

The title of this page is certainly ironic, since the last thing that this text intends is to provide instructions to the reader, or to give advice. What it wants is precisely not to be consumed. That is why this "user's manual" must be rejected after it has been read. What is intended is that the reader make use of the texts as he or she wishes. But that they be transformed, preferably, into part of the dialogues of which the reader participates. It is true that the text is discursive: as is, unfortunately, every text. But it does not want to be so. This is only one of the several contradictions that the reader shall find along the course of the reading. But such contradictions are inevitable: the text wishes to be a mirror to the human situation.

2

THE GROUND WE TREAD

It is not necessary to have a keen ear in order to find out that the steps we take toward the future sound hollow. But it is necessary to have concentrated hearing if one wishes to find out which type of vacuity resonates with our progress. There are several types of vacuity, and ours must be compared to others, if the aim is to understand it. The incomparable is incomprehensible. If we affirm that our situation is incomparable, we give up the effort to grasp it.

The comparison that imposes itself is to the vacuity of the Baroque. There are innumerable traces in the present that evoke the Baroque. We bear the mark of the same somber rationalism (logics, informatics, cybernetics), and of the same magic and fanatic irrationalism (mass media, phantastic ideologies). But there is a decisive difference. During the Baroque humanity advanced toward the future over a stage. All of its gestures, even the most sincere, were marked by theatricality. The vacuity that resonated under its feet was of the void under the stage. Baroque man represented.[1] For example, he represented faith in waging

---

1 In Portuguese *representar* also means "to act" or "to play a role."

3

religious wars. Baroque vacuity was the consequence of a medieval *loss of faith in dogmas*. Our vacuity is different. We do not represent anything. Our world is not a stage. We are not actors, and if we act, it is not to represent a drama, but to divert the audience's attention and our own from the subjects that really matter. We act like criminals that try to hide their tracks. We pretend. Our progress is a farce. The vacuity under our feet is not Baroque. We have not lost our faith in dogmas: *we have lost faith in ourselves*. We are as *counter-reformists* as was the Baroque (we want to cover up the recent revolution with warm cloths), but for different reasons.

Although comparable with the Baroque, in certain aspects, our situation is in fact incomparable to any other. That is because an incomparable, unheard of, never before seen event happened recently, which emptied the ground we tread. *Auschwitz.* Other posterior events; Hiroshima, the Gulags, are nothing but variations of the first. Therefore every attempt to grasp the present leads to the following questions: how was Auschwitz possible? How can we live after this? Such questions relate not only to the ones directly or indirectly responsible, and not only to those who were directly or indirectly hit by it: they relate to everyone who takes part in our culture. Because what is so incomparable, unheard of, never before seen and therefore incomprehensible in Auschwitz, is that it was there that Western culture revealed one of its inherent virtualities. Auschwitz is a *characteristic realization* of our culture.

It is neither the product of a particular Western ideology, nor of specific "advanced" industrial techniques.

It springs directly from the depths of culture and of its concepts and values. The possibility to realize Auschwitzes is implicit within our culture from the very start: the Western "project" already harbored it, although as a remote possibility. Auschwitz lies within the initial *program* of the West, which progressively realizes all of its virtualities as history unfolds. That is why the question that Auschwitz poses before us is not: how did it happen? It serves no purpose to "explain" Auschwitz. The fundamental question is: how was it *possible*? Because what is being questioned is not the extermination camp, but the West. Thus one other question: how to live within a culture henceforth unmasked?

Everything that happened afterward resonates with such a question, with such vacuity. Every economic, social, political, technical, scientific, artistic, philosophic event is corroded by such an undigested question. The distance that separates us from the event does not mitigate the abyss, it erodes it even deeper. Because the distance progressively dissolves the aura of the horror that envelops the event, and it progressively opens up a vision of the scene. It progressively reveals that at Auschwitz all of our categories, all of our "models," suffered an irreparable shipwreck. Auschwitz was a *revolutionary* event, in the sense that it overthrew our culture. Insofar as we seek ways to cover up such revolution with trips to the moon or with genetic manipulations, we are counter-revolutionaries: we are inverting the course of history in order to cover up the past.

The unspoken in Auschwitz is not the mass murder, it is *not* the *crime*. It is the ultimate *reification* of people into amorphous objects, into ashes. The Western tendency toward objectification was finally realized and it was done so in the shape of an *apparatus*.[2] The SS were functionaries of an extermination apparatus, and their victims functioned in function of their own annihilation. The extermination camp's program, once it started functioning, developed in an automatic fashion, autonomous from the decisions of the initial programmers, even if it contributed to the defeat of the programmers, as it effectively did. The SS and the Jews functioned in function of each other, like cogwheels. The models for such functionality were provided by the highest of Western values: the SS behaved like "heroes" and the Jews like "martyrs." This is an apparatus that functions at a borderline situation: objective even beyond death.

What has just been said is *intolerable*. We cannot accept it and so we mobilize arguments against it. Good arguments. The SS behaved like criminals: they removed the gold teeth from the cadavers. The Jews behaved like victims: they rose up in the Warsaw ghetto. Such arguments are true, but they do not reach the nucleus, the "*eidos*" of the phenomenon: they do not grasp it. Although there was "normal" behavior (theft, murder, revolt, heroism), there was also "abnormal" behavior: functionality during a borderline situation. And this is what counts. There,

---

2 When using the term "apparatus" in English, Flusser always used the term in its Latin form for both the singular and plural forms. In English it is possible to use both apparatus and apparatuses for the plural, but since Flusser opted to use apparatus as the plural in all of the texts that he wrote in English, I decided to retain the same form for the translations in order to keep the translated texts as close as possible in style to his own English texts. [TN]

for the first time in the history of humanity, an apparatus was put into operation that was programmed with the most advanced techniques available, which realized the objectification of man, together with the functional collaboration of man.

The previous horrors committed by Western society against other societies and against itself (and there are many) were *crimes*. They were violations of Western models of behavior: anti-Christian, anti-human, irrational. Thus it is possible to condemn them and continue to be Western, even if the horror is so colossal, such as the enslavement of Africans. However, it is not possible to condemn Auschwitz and continue to adhere consciously to the West. Auschwitz is not a violation of Western models of behavior, it is, on the contrary, the *result of the application* of such models. Our culture allowed its mystifying mask to fall at Auschwitz and revealed its real face. The face of a monster that objectifies man. Our culture has shown that it must be rejected *in toto* if we admit that the purpose of every culture is to allow for the convivial existence of men that recognize each other mutually as subjects.

However: it is not possible to reject one's own culture. It is the *ground we tread.* Those who seek to reject their own culture (as Nietzsche did in rejecting Judeo-Christianity), fall victim to madness. Those who reject their culture's models are incapable of grasping the world in which they live. Cultural models are traps to catch the world. Those who seek to substitute their own models for others' (for example by shouting "Hare Krishna") will find that such exotic models have already been caught by the very models to be substituted. There is no exit: we are condemned to use our models and to serve such models, even after they have been unmasked, if we wish to continue living. The only alternative would be to commit suicide. That is: we must continue our economic, political, scientific, artistic, philosophic activities despite Auschwitz. *We must continue progressing despite everything.*

That is why there are those who recommend that we should seek to forget what happened, that we should repress the event. They maintain that enough has already been said and written about the subject and that it is time to "overcome" it. But such an ostrich strategy reveals itself to be disastrous. Because the result is that Auschwitz transfers itself from the Poland of the 1940s to the post-industrial society of the future. What characterizes the extermination camp is precisely that it is not an event that can be "overcome," because it is the *first realization* of an inherent virtuality within the Western project, which will repeat itself in other formats unless we become totally conscious of it. The advantage (if this is an appropriate term) that Auschwitz offers us, is to give us a concrete example of the West's tendency toward the apparatus. For the first time in our history it is possible for us to experience concretely the *utopia inherent* in our culture. For the first time in our history we have the experience that utopia, no matter in what form, toward which we progress, is the extermination camp.

Everywhere we can observe, as of now, the emergence of variations on the theme "Auschwitz." Everywhere apparatus spring, just like mushrooms after a Nazi rain, from the ground that has become rotten. Certainly: such new apparatus are not externally similar to the Nazi extermination camps. Their labels are different, as are the ideologies that pretend to inspire them. Even the apparatus that admittedly envision extermination, such as the Gulags, the ones of a future nuclear war, or the ones that functioned in Vietnam, claim to be different from Auschwitz. Others claim to be "friends of mankind," such as the scientific, technical and administrative apparatus. But such labels and such ideologies are deceptive and serve only to cover up the essence of apparatus. They are all just like Auschwitz, black boxes that function with complex inner-workings in order to realize a program. They all function according to an *inertia* that is inherent to them and such functionality *escapes*, from a certain point, *the control* of their initial programmers. In a final analysis such apparatus function, all of them, toward the annihilation of all their functionaries, including their programmers. Exactly because they objectify and dehumanize man.

Thus Western culture reveals itself as a project that seeks to transform itself into an apparatus. What characterizes the West is its capacity for an objectifying transcendence. Such transcendence allows for the transformation of all phenomena, including the human phenomenon, into an object of knowledge and manipulation. The space for such transcendence opened up thanks to Judeo-Christianity and resulted, in the course of our history, in science, technique, and recently in Auschwitz. The ultimate objectification of the Jews into ashes is the ultimate victory of the spirit of the West. It is *social technique* taken to the extreme. Certainly: the transformation of men into ashes is a primitive, incipient social technique that

9

progressively refines itself. It will be followed by less brutal objectifications, such as the robotization of society. But it does not matter which form it will assume: it will always be an objectifying manipulation of mankind. Although the apparatus of the immediate future are not necessarily incineration ovens, all will be, and not only the nuclear ones, apparatus for the annihilation of man.

The Western program contains several virtualities, not only apparatus. Numerous virtualities have not yet been realized. In this sense the "history of the West" has not yet ended, the Western game continues. But all unrealized virtualities are infected by apparatus. This is why it has currently become *impossible to engage ourselves in the "progress of culture."* As doing so would be to engage ourselves in our own annihilation. We have lost faith in our culture, in the ground we tread. That is: we have lost faith in ourselves. It is this hollow vibration that follows our steps toward the future. What remains is for us to analyze the event "Auschwitz" in all its details in order to discover the fundamental project that realized itself there for the first time, so that we may nurture the hope to project ourselves out of that project. Out of the history of the West. This is the "post-historical" climate in which we are condemned to live in from hereon.

OUR SKY

The *Copernican revolution* changed our religious experience. It dislocated the Earth from the center of the universe and from then on abolished the heavens that until then had enveloped and protected humanity. It turned the skies astronomical and no longer religious. And it created another religious heaven: a heaven that is no longer "above" but "beyond." This is why space travel will not have a religious impact, unless we manage to incorporate the experience according to which the terms "high" and "low" have their meaning restricted to bodies and become meaningless in empty space. If we manage to absorb the relativity of the meaning of such terms, we will have relativized the meaning of derivate terms like "infernal" and "sublime," which will still have an impact on religious experience.

Astronomy is no longer opposed to religion, as it was in the Renaissance. In the same way that none of the natural sciences are still opposed to religion. The quarrel surrounding Darwinism was the last one of this kind. The reason for this is that both terms "faith" and "knowledge" have had a change in meaning. *Faith* no longer means "belief" but *trust*. And knowledge no longer *means* to have indubitable information, but *information worthy of trust*. The problems of faith are no longer of the type: "could this be true?" but of the type: "can I trust this?" And the propositions of science, that preferential fountain of knowledge of ours, no longer pretend to be indubitable. On the contrary, if they are, then they are not considered to be scientific. These propositions pretend to be worthy of trust precisely for being "falsifiable." This implies that faith and knowledge no longer occupy conflicting positions within our conscience: they occupy complementary positions. We have faith in science and we accept that the experience of faith is one of the fountains of knowledge. Such complementarity is, however, dangerous for both religion and science: both relativize each other. Both dilute themselves and both are in crisis. Both faith and knowledge are in danger: a crisis of trust.

Example: when I lie in my bed I "know" that the bed is a swarm of particles that float in empty space. Nevertheless I trust the solidity of the bed. Such trust of mine in the solidity of the objective world that surrounds me is not, however, anti-scientific: on the contrary, it makes it possible for science to work. The knowledge of atomic structures does not undermine my trust in the solidity of objects, but it undermines, yes, my trust in the scientific propositions that project a hollow universe, therefore existentially inaccessible. Simultaneously, such propositions undermine my trust in religious discourse, which projects a solid universe. Thus the current complementarity of faith and knowledge erodes the trust in both.

Religious people may object that the chosen example relates to a vague trust, but not to religious faith. For such people, religious faith, to be precise, is not the trust in the world of objects, but in a transcendental foundation that goes beyond the world of objects. Religious faith in this case would be precisely the piercing of the objective world toward a transcendental one. Such an objection would be a mistake. There are, certainly, religious experiences that thus pierce the world of objects and reveal it as a "deceptive appearance" that covers up "reality." But such experiences are not characteristic of Western religiosity. Our religiosity, as it pierces the world of objects, reveals that world to be "real" in the sense of it being a "Divine creation." The transcendence revealed by Western religiosity is a space that supports the objective world and that increases the trust in it. It allows space for knowledge and manipulation of the objective world. It is the space within which "theories" are made and from which "techniques" are applied to the world, to objects. Thus Western faith implies trust in the solidity of the objective world. *This trust is part of Western faith.* From this point of view there is no crisis in Western faith: all of us, unless we are mad, nurture a trust in the solidity of objects. And if the current complementarity between faith and knowledge erodes our trust in general, this is a symptom of how much religion and science rest on the same foundation. We are neither Pre-Socratics, nor Buddhists, and we cannot be either.

But religious people are correct on one point: religious faith is not only trust in the solidity of objects. It is also and above all *trust in other men and in oneself.* In the West,

13

"God" is the method by which one loves the Other as one loves oneself. The religious experience of the West reveals God in the human face. With effect: this is the only image that we have of God – man is His image. To love God *above all else* means precisely to love the Other and oneself. There is no other method to love God, and not even another method to overcome things. Thus Western religious experience implies trust in objects and *beyond that*, trust in man as the image of God. And so now we are obliged to accept the crisis of faith: it has now become impossible to have trust in man.

It could be possible to think that this loss of faith in man is the result of scientific anthropologies, for example of Freudianism, which reveal man to be a being unworthy of trust and therefore, to think of a conflict between science and faith, despite everything. But this would be a mistake. Such anthropologies are not the cause but one of the effects of the crisis of trust. The cause of the loss of faith in man is not our knowledge about him, but our concrete experience with him, with others and with ourselves. The experiences accumulated by this and past generations, demonstrate, beyond any reasonable doubt, that man is unworthy of trust, that it would be *insanity to trust him.*

"God is dead," not because we now know more than past generations, but because we killed Him by the acts we have committed. Our grandparents, our parents and even we have committed acts of which Auschwitz is a prototype, and which are unquestionable proof that it would be insanity to want to love the Other. Acts that prove that man is an object of manipulation and knowledge.

As the technical manipulation of man becomes routine, it becomes wholly insincere to wish to recognize in man the image of God. At the moment it would *even* be madness not to have trust in objects, but it *already is* madness to have trust in man. This is the death of God, the real crisis in religiosity and therefore the crisis in everything that springs from such religiosity: from Western culture.

It is not, therefore, a case of an opposition between faith and knowledge, but of a *crisis of trust in man, including human knowledge.* Scientific presuppositions (its implicit "theory of knowledge") deserve as little trust as the dogmas of established religions. Both are "unbelievable." But in the case of dogmas, the following is happening: the less believable they are, the more welcome they become to certain levels of society. That is: to those who have become aware of how difficult it is to live without trust in the Other and without self-confidence. The more unbelievable the dogmas become, the higher is the sacrifice of "reason," and therefore more "worthy" the return to churches and synagogues. It is a case of "reconquering faith," of reconquering trust and of entering faith through the backdoor.

Recently a similar phenomenon has been observed in relation to scientific knowledge. Its pretension toward an "exemption of values," toward objectivity, have become unbelievable, and several scientists are prepared to sacrifice their "critical sense" in order to save objective knowledge. They seek to preserve the trust in scientific knowledge through a religious attitude. Science is currently in a phase in which it is becoming religious, it is becoming one among many established religions. The current religious crisis, and that of trust, is mixing science with established religions.

If looked at superficially, the current religious situation presents itself as complex. A certain elite seeks to "re-conquer faith" in order to re-conquer trust in man. Other members of the elite seek to at least re-conquer trust in scientific knowledge. And the great majority suffers the decadence of trust in a passive and somewhat unconscious way, executing the gestures of trust in religions and in science in the form of ritual, since they have been programmed for this by mass culture. But if seen from even closer, the current religious situation is extremely simple. The trust in man, therefore in God, and in an "objectifying" transcendence is becoming unsustainable. God has died and Western religiosity, the ground we tread, is becoming hollow.

This explains the attempts by so many individuals to escape our culture and seek salvation in exotic lands, and in many ways, lands of fantasy, or in "cults." These are desperate acts. Because it is not a case of the current crisis of trust, of *doubt* in relation to the "ontological dignity" of man, as if we were not certain whether man is or is not the image of God. It is a case of *certainty*: that man is a manipulable object. Because faith can live perfectly well together with doubt and with effect, it can be stated that faith cannot live without doubt. But certainty kills faith, because certainty is despair. Hence, not a single strategy, not even the one of escapism, is able to save faith today.

The preferred example of how certainty kills faith is provided by the current crisis of science. Science can be considered as methodic doubt, so much so that trust in its enunciations incorporates doubt as essential. But when the certainty that scientific knowledge is "impossible" emerges (for example: that it doesn't reach concrete experiences), when skepticism emerges, trust in science ceases. The despair of skepticism ends the trust in science just as the despair in man ends with religious faith. Further proof of how much science is nothing but one among the religions currently in crisis. Our despair in relation to man, our certainty in relation to him, is killing God, that is: killing all forms of trust.

What remains are desperate acts. Attempts to escape toward nothingness. In this sense religion's heaven and astronomy's space are, finally, the same abyss. We throw ourselves toward "transcendence" in the same way that we throw ourselves toward interplanetary space in order to escape the abyss that has opened underneath the ground we tread. And just like the concepts "high" and "low," and their derivate terms "sublime" and "infernal," have come to have relative meanings, it makes no difference if we judge this act of throwing ourselves to be either "sublimation" or "extreme alienation." It makes no difference if today our acts are interpreted as "progress" or "decadence."

In a certain way we may state that our time is once again "Catholic" just as it was in the Counter-Reformation. We are "Catholics" in the sense that there is currently a common sense (kat holos), conscious or unconscious, in relation to the ontological position of man. He is a groundless being and a being that can be objectified. Within this consensus nests a specific negative religiosity, the mirror of Western religiosity. Contrary to our naively atheist parents, we are profoundly religious, although perversely so. However, it is questionable whether our profound religious experience is solace.

Our Program

The notion that the world and human existence are *programmed* is relatively new. Several implicit aspects of this notion have not yet entered our consciousness. Our mystical heritage has accustomed us to the notion of a world and an existence governed by *destiny*, and the natural sciences have awakened in us the notion of a world and existence governed by *causality*. Present times demand that we rethink such notions of destiny, of causality, and of programming.

Our religious tradition and the mystical, foundational experiences that hide behind it, project an image according to which humans and the world within which they exist, are subjected to a purpose that demands an aim. The obscurity of the purpose and the opacity of the aim open up the field to the mysterious human capacity to oppose both. Although impenetrable, the problematic implicit in such an image is familiar. The natural sciences, opposed to this tradition, project a different image according to which every event is the effect of specific causes, which are in turn causes of specific effects. Experience presents itself in this image as being part of a complex net of causal chains.

Currently both images are becoming unbearable. They reveal themselves to be naive extrapolations of a concrete situation that could be referred to as "programmatic." The unbearable nature of both images is due, on the one hand, to epistemological considerations, and on the other hand, to recent political experiences. Both factors point to naive ideologies from which these images are projected.

In the *finalistic* image of predestination, the central problem is that of human freedom. Can man oppose his destiny with free will, and if so to what extent can he do this? This is a question of the possibility of the emancipation of man from the "reasons" that drive him, or from the question of "sin." This is because the finalistic image is a political vision tinted with ethics. One of its extremes is fatalism and the other is arbitrariness.

In the *causal* image, the problem of freedom emerges differently. This image is an apolitical vision that has an a-ethical, mechanist tint and in both its extremes, which are determinism and chaos, it excludes the possibility of freedom. But this image also allows for a notion of "subjective" freedom: given the impenetrable complexity of causes and the unpredictability of effects in every given event, it is possible to act as if action were free, even though it is "objectively" determined.

In the *programmatic* image it seems, until now, impossible even to formulate the problem of freedom. The term does not appear to have meaning within this novel context. Some examples will illuminate the difficulty here:

Finalistic *cosmology* considers the universe to be a situation that represents a stage in the progress toward another, final, previously understood stage. Causal

20

cosmology considers the universe to be a situation that emerged out of previous situations from necessity, and will thus necessarily produce future situations as its consequence. Programmatic cosmology considers the universe to be a situation in which particular and inherent virtualities - part of the universe since its origin - have realized themselves by chance, while other virtualities - that will be realized by chance in the future - remain, as yet unrealized.

Finalistic *anthropology* considers man to be an evolved being, because he is closer to the aim of biological evolution. Causal anthropology sees man as one of the species from the primate branch, a link in the causal chain that structures biological process. Programmatic anthropology sees in man one of the possible permutations of the genetic information that is common to all living beings.

Finalistic *ethology* considers human behavior to be a series of motivated movements. Causal ethology sees in human behavior a series of reflexes to external and internal causes. Programmatic ethology sees in human behavior casual manifestations of the virtualities inherent in man and his environment.

If we consider the models applied within these fields from a programmatic perspective, we will find that the second principle of thermodynamics (according to which the universe is an entropic process) applies to its cosmology. In anthropology, molecular biology (according to which the structure of particular nucleic acids contain all possible organic forms) applies. In ethology, analytic psychology (according to which human behavior manifests particular virtualities contained within the subconscious) applies. And if we extend the programmatic image to other fields (logic, linguistics, sociology, economy, politology, etc.), we will find everywhere that all models are of the same type: they are programs.

What characterizes programs is the fact that they are systems in which chance becomes necessity. They are games in which every virtuality, even the least probable, will be realized of necessity if the game is played for a sufficiently long time. The least probable structures, such as planetary systems, emerge necessarily during the course of the evolution of the program contained in the Big Bang, according to the second law of thermodynamics. But they emerge by chance at a particular moment. Absurdly improbable structures, such as the human brain, emerge necessarily in the course of the evolution of the program contained in genetic information, even though they had been entirely unpredictable in the amoeba. And they emerge by chance at a particular moment. Wonderful artworks such as *The Marriage of Figaro* emerge necessarily in the course of the evolution of the program contained in the initial project of Western culture. Although it is absurd to look for them in that initial project, for example, in Ancient Greek music. This is because although they have become necessary, such realizations emerge by chance in the course of the game.

The fundamental concept from the programmatic perspective is, therefore, *chance*. This is what is new. For finalistic thought, chance does not exist: what seems to be chance is in fact a purpose as yet undiscovered. Chance plays an even lesser role for causal thought: what seems to be chance is in fact a cause that has yet to be discovered. But for programmatic thought, what happens is the opposite. What seems to be a purpose, and what seems to be a cause are, in fact, only naively interpreted chance occurrences. Finalistic thought is naive because it looks for purposes behind chance in order to endow them with meaning. Causal thought is naive because it looks for causes behind chance in order to organize them. In effect, programs seem like purposes if looked at anthropomorphically and they seem like causes if looked at mechanistically. Thus, from a programmatic perspective, finalistic thought is revealed to be an ideology that anthropomorphizes and causal thought an ideology that objectifies. The programmatic perspective seeks to put these ideologies "within parentheses" and to accept chance as the concrete given structure that it is. The Programmatic perspective is the *point of view of the absurd*.

Currently, programmatic thought imposes itself everywhere. Both natural as well as cultural *sciences* tend to show that every finalistic and causal "explanation" is condemned to failure. Finalistic explanations have failed because they explain the present according to the future, that is, the concrete according to the abstraction "not yet." And causal explanations have failed because they explain the present according to the past, that is, the concrete according to the abstraction "no longer." It is possible to observe the same imposition of programmatic thought within the *arts*. Every current tendency demonstrates that reality is progressively experienced as an absurd game of chance, as a "happening." But it is above all in the field of *politics* that the imposition of programmatic thought reveals its essence. If society's behavior is progressively experienced and interpreted as absurdly programmed by programs without aim or purpose, the problem of freedom, which is the problem of politics, becomes inconceivable. From a programmatic perspective, politics, and therefore history, comes to an end.

Before the advent of a programmatic reality, it was possible for one to live simultaneously with both finalistic and causal realities, even though they are contradictory. It was possible to apply a causal perspective to nature and a finalistic perspective to culture. Nature could be objectified and culture anthropomorphized. Natural science could be "hard" and cultural science "soft." This was possible because both perspectives have an identical linear structure: "purpose-aim" and "cause-effect." The same does not happen from a programmatic point of view, which has multiple dimensions. Final and causal linearity are but two dimensions of programmatic reality. The programmatic image absorbs both preceding images and transforms them. The difficulty with the programmatic image is precisely this "imperialism:" it does not allow any other image to stand alongside it.

This certainly is an epistemological and aesthetic challenge, but it is above all as a political challenge that the concept of a programmatic reality is difficult to digest. Here, it is about the question of freedom, of the emancipation of man from the intentions of other men. In politics, therefore, finalistic thought is the only appropriate thought. The challenge that a programmatic reality represents is the need to *learn* to think apolitically, if we want to preserve the concept of human freedom.

This is a paradox. If we continue to think politically, finalistically, if we continue to seek for purposes behind the programs that govern us, we will fall fatal victims to this absurd programming, which precisely predicts just such attempts at "demythologizing" among its virtualities.

We can always better observe how different apparatus progressively program individual and social behavior. And we can observe, on top of this, the behavior of "intelligent instruments," whose program we know and in which we recognize our own behavior. That is: we can always better observe how much the programmatic reality becomes progressively less "theoretical" and is increasingly applied within praxis. Certainly it is a case of deliberate application. There are programmers. However, despite this: if we persist with finalistic thought, if we continue to try to discover the programmers behind the programs, in order to demystify their intentions, we will lose sight of what is essential in the scene. Within the current scene all "Kulturkritik" is an anachronism. Because what is essential in the scene is the fact that programs, despite being projected by programmers, become autonomous. *Apparatus always function increasingly independently from their programmer's intentions.* And apparatus that are programmed by other apparatus emerge with increasing frequency. Their initial purpose always recedes farther beyond the horizon, and becomes less interesting. Human programming is itself increasingly programmed by apparatus. Certainly: some specific programmers judge themselves, subjectively, to be "owners" of the decisions taken by apparatus. When, in reality, they are nothing but functionaries who are programmed to think of themselves in this way. "Kulturkritik" naively accepts the programmer's naive and programmed view, and in so doing, itself becomes a function within programs. Apparatus incorporate both programmers and critics progressively. Freedom will die if we continue to think politically and to act according to such thinking.

We must *neither anthropomorphize nor objectify apparatus*. We must grasp them in their cretinous concreteness, in their programmed and absurd functionality, in order to be able to comprehend them and thus insert them into meta-programs. The paradox is that such meta-programs are equally absurd games. In sum: what we must learn is to accept the absurd, if we wish to emancipate ourselves from functionalism. Freedom is conceivable only as an absurd game with apparatus, as a game with programs. It is conceivable only after we have accepted politics and human existence in general to be an absurd game. Whether we continue to be "men" or become robots depends on how fast we learn to play: we can become players of the game or pieces in it.

OUR WORK

The shift from agrarian to industrial society had *ontological* effects. The farmer experiences reality differently from the worker. The current shift from industrial to post-industrial society will have comparable effects. The worker experiences reality differently from the functionary.

Agriculture is the patient manipulation of animate nature. *Industry* is the violent manipulation of inanimate nature: it forces it to reformulate itself according to models. The farmer waits so that animal and plant develop, under his care, in a way that is useful for him. The engineer forces raw material to be as it should be according to his projects. For the farmer, reality is an animate being put under his care. For the engineer, reality is a material to be hammered, burnt and gasified. This ontology, born out of praxis, also extends to other men. For the farmer, the Other is a serf whom he must care for, or a type of cattle. For the factory owner, the Other is a worker that must be molded according to preconceived models, as a type of mass. Men that are thus inserted within the dominant ontology, become themselves according to it. The serf becomes the herd and accepts the dominant class as shepherds. The worker becomes the mass and the dominant class the hammer.

The shift from agrarian to industrial society substituted the Aristotelian vision of an animated cosmos for a scientific view of the world. This implies a reformulation of the meaning of *theory*. For the agrarian society, theory is the concept of immutable forms, for example: the form of the cow and of wheat. For industrial society, theory is the elaboration of mutable forms, for example: the form of the hammer and the shoe. Experience, as well as concept and action, have been modified by the shift from one type of society to another.

In agrarian society there were craftsmen, and in industrial society there were country peasants. And although their praxis was dissonant from the dominant one, they were still subjected to the dominant ontology. The blacksmith hammered the sickle in view of the wheat, and the country peasant milked the cow in view of the milk bottle. The agrarian blacksmith hammered in function of an animate cosmos, and the industrial peasant milked cows in function of an inanimate cosmos. And in both societies there were also administrators. In the agrarian society the Church was dominant and in the industrial society it was the State. In both cases the administrators were also subjected to the dominant ontology: the Church administered herds and the State the masses.

The current shift from industrial to *post-industrial* society can be minimized in order to avoid that we become aware of the ontological revolution currently underway. It could be said that it is only a case of proportional modification of the types of work in society. In which case, for the agrarian society the majority would consist of farmers, the minority of craftsmen, and an insignificant minority of administrators. For the industrial society the majority would consist of workers, the minority of farmers, and an insignificant minority of administrators. For the post-industrial society the majority would consist of administrative functionaries ("services" and "white collar workers"), the minority of workers, and an insignificant minority of farmers.

However, this minimization effort is doomed to failure. Because a proportional modification changes all forms of work, including the minor ones. Industrial society industrialized agriculture and administration. The post-industrial society progressively functionalizes industry and agriculture. But what this minimization intends to obscure is the fact that such a transformation of this type of work modifies the dominant ontology, and therefore society's experience, vision and action. In order for us to grasp the new ontology that formulates itself, it is necessary for us to consider its source: the *functionary's praxis*.

The functionary sits behind a desk and receives papers covered with *symbols* (letters and algorithms), which are sent to him by other functionaries. He archives these papers and covers others with similar symbols, in order to send them to other functionaries still. The functionary receives symbols, stores symbols, produces symbols and emits symbols. He does it partially via manual methods and partially via cybernetic apparatus of the type "word processors." His praxis happens within a context referred to as "the codified world."

Symbols are phenomena that have been consciously, semi-consciously, or unconsciously conventionalized in order to have *meanings*; they are "decipherable" to those who participate in the convention that established them. Logic distinguishes between two types of symbols, the "observational" ones, whose meanings are concrete phenomena, and the "theoretical" ones, whose meanings are other symbols. And logic affirms that theoretical symbols can be reduced to observational symbols, unless they are "empty" symbols. Thus logic affirms that the functionary's praxis can be reduced to the concrete world, unless it is an "empty" praxis. Therefore, in a final analysis, the functionary's praxis seeks, as every praxis does, to modify the concrete world.

This interpretation of functional praxis is a *mistake* that could be verified by an observation of functionalism: The apparatus, within which the functionaries function, dispose of slots or openings, for "output." For example, there are counters at which the papers covered by symbols are delivered to concrete people ("physical," as it is said symptomatically). Passports, for example, according to a logical analysis, would signify the bearer, the concrete person. But for the functionary, the passport emitter, *the vector of signification has been inverted*. The concrete person, the passport receiver, is the one that signifies the passport. The person is the symbol and the passport is the meaning. The person signifies the number in the passport. The functionary's reality is the passport, and the person is what gives "meaning" to the passport. This inversion of vectors of signification characterizes functionalism: its praxis does not seek to modify the concrete world, but the codified world.

For the functionary, the codified world is reality "*tout court,*" because it is within it that his career and his life occur. The way in which he manipulates the symbols decides if the apparatus will employ him, if he advances and how he will retire. The way in which he functions with symbols will provide him his salary, his holidays, his leisure, in sum: his *rights*. The functionary does not expect from the apparatus that it will modify the concrete world, but that it will provide him his rights. That is why symbols are not for the functionary what they are for the logician: phenomena that have been conventionalized in order to have meaning. They are, for him, reality proper. Every ontology that was different from this one would be for him alienating.

For the farmer, "to live" means to care for live nature, to occupy the "just" place within the order of the animate cosmos. The farmer rebels if such a place, reserved for him, is denied. The farmer is *conservative* according to the dominant ontology. For the worker, "to live" means to relish in the result of his work, the product. When he discovers that part of the result, the "surplus value," is denied him, he seeks to establish a fair distribution of the available goods. The worker is *revolutionary* according to the dominant ontology. For the functionary, "to live," means to function within an apparatus that provides him his rights. If the apparatus denies him his rights, it is because it has been badly programmed and is malfunctioning. So it must be fixed. For the functionary, rights are not ethical or political judgments, they are formal judgments. The functionary is *formalist* according to the dominant ontology. In the post-industrial society it makes no sense to try to distinguish between conservatism and revolution, between right and left: Politics loses all meaning.

This seems to indicate that the post-industrial society will be a bureaucracy, a society in which the functionary is dominant. But everything indicates that this is a mistake. Because on the contrary: *wherever there is bureaucracy, the post-industrial society is not yet well programmed.* So everything indicates that functional programs will dominate the post-industrial society, within which the functionaries will function progressively more like invisible cogwheels inside the black boxes. This will be *technocracy*. Functionaries are not comparable to the farmers and factory owners of preceding societies, but to the serfs and workers. The apparent dominant class shall be the programmers, although an attentive analysis will also reveal that they too are specialized functionaries. The apparatus will form the real dominant class. It will be an inhuman society.

Nevertheless: programmers are "new men," a type of men that did not exist in previous societies. They assume themselves players of programs, for whom what counts is not the modification of the world but the game. Reality for them is the game of functionalism. The symbols that they manipulate in order to project programs, signify functionalism. Every attempt to seek a "transcendent reality" of functionalism is for them metaphysics in the bad meaning of the term. Only the symbols can be so expressed, and their ultimate meaning is *ex definitione* unutterable. And what cannot be said must be silent. By their praxis, programmers are born neo-positivists. For them, "to live" is to participate in an absurd game. And that is their lifestyle.

This programmatic ontology leads to the invention of computers and intelligent instruments, and to the transformation of society into a cybernetic system composed of functionaries and apparatus. For programmers, man is a functionary to be programmed to live in a symbolic context. Man is a being that is to be symbolized, for example, enumerated. Men are cyphers to be inserted into several formal games, for example statistics or perforated cards. Although the post-industrial society has not yet been effectively realized, we can observe everywhere how it is emerging. And we already have its models: Eichmann as model functionary, Kissinger as model programmer, and Auschwitz as post-industrial society.

However, the programmers, these "new men," have not yet become fully conscious of the ontology that sustains them. If we observe how they program, we will observe that they are not always aware that *they are themselves programmed to program*. The ontology that is dominating society functions, at the moment, only at the level of experience and has not yet been formalized. What is still missing for us is the equivalent of an Aristotle of the agrarian society and a Kant of the industrial society. What is urgent is to rethink the meaning of the term *theory* in this new context.

For the agrarian society, "theory" was the vision of immutable forms. For the industrial society, "theory" was the elaboration of ever-new models. In the post-industrial society, "theory" will very probably be a game strategy. We already have a whole series of disciplines that are "theories" in this new meaning of the term: informatics, cybernetics, and decision theory to mention only a few examples. These disciplines are derived from logic and from Greek mathematics, and reformulate these "theories" in order to adapt them to the functional context. Without a doubt, other theories of this type will emerge in the future.

But what counts is the awareness that strategies are applicable only when game rules apply; that rules are conventions, which order the manipulation of symbols, and that both rules as well as symbols demand consensus. Therefore, every ontology that accepts the codified world as real, must accept consensus as a source. And that the radical reality for such an ontology is necessarily *human intersubjectivity*. Once we become fully conscious of this (there are already symptoms that this is happening), it will become conceivable that the post-industrial society will not necessarily be a totalitarianism of apparatus, but possibly a society that elaborates programs in function of consensus. But for sure: such utopian vision of a dialogic society runs against the experiences we have with apparatus. For the time being, it is they who program us for consensus.

Our Knowledge

There are several different tendencies that can be distinguished in the history of science. The most obvious one is the quantitative: we always know more in relation to an increasing number of subjects. But there are also the less obvious, qualitative tendencies. For example there is a thesis according to which scientific knowledge becomes *progressively less satisfactory*, so that the lessening of satisfaction can serve as a measure for progress. A particular knowledge is said to be "satisfactory" when it answers a specific question. Completely satisfactory explanations exhaust all questions, so that there is nothing left to ask.

The following propositions may be compared: "God created the world so that man may live in it" and "the world emerged approximately 13.75 billion years ago from the Big Bang." Both propositions deal with the same subject, the origin of the world, but they are answers to different questions. The first asks: "*for what* did the world emerge?" and the second, "*how* did it emerge?" This thesis affirms that the gap that lies between the two propositions (the history of science) is characterized by the reformulation of questions. At the beginning of history there would have been questions that start with "for what?" and would have been followed by questions that start with "why?" and "how?" These are questions with an end: causal and formal (the ones that were referred to as "programmatic" in the last essay). According to this thesis, the first proposition would be the "finalistic explanation" and the second the "programmatic explanation."

Within the interval that lies between "God" and the "Big Bang" (between the sixth century B.C. and now), *finalistic explanations* would have been progressively eliminated from the scientific discourse, for the curious reason of being too satisfactory. They exhaust all questions and do not allow for others to be formulated. If I explain: "it rains so that the road will be wet," it leaves me nothing to ask about the rain. Thus finalistic explanations represent an interruption in the flux of the discourse. And in this sense they are not "good questions." Currently they have been practically eliminated from the discourse of almost all of the natural sciences, although within the field of biology they are more difficult to eradicate. However, finalistic questions are characteristic of political discourse to this day, or in other words, of the cultural sciences.

For the natural sciences such questions have been substituted by *causal* ones, which has made the discourse of these sciences extraordinarily dynamic, so that it always flows with violent speed toward new explanations. But the price of such progressiveness has been high. If I explain: "animals see because they have eyes," instead of: "animals have eyes in order to see," I have a sensation of dissatisfaction, of having somehow betrayed the phenomenon "animal" with which the explanations deal. This lack of satisfaction becomes even more obvious if I try to substitute finalistic explanations with causal ones within the field of the cultural sciences – as it has been done since the 19th century. If I apply a causal explanation: "the thief steals because he suffered a trauma during childhood," instead of a finalistic one: "he steals with the aim of getting richer," I verify what the reformulation of the question implies. Causal explanations *eliminate* one of the dimensions implicit in finalistic explanations, that is: value judgment. The universe of causal explanations is value exempt. Within it, it makes no sense to ask about motives." That is why the discourse of causal explanations is less satisfactory than the finalistic one: because of the relative poverty of its universe of signification.

Ultimately, science sees itself obliged to give up causal explanations within several fields and to substitute them for *formal* ones. If, for example, I project an isolated photon against a screen with two slots, it is not "good" if I ask: "why does the photon go through one of the slots and not the other?" The "good" question is: "*how* does the photon travel?" This necessity to substitute causal questions by formal ones becomes even more painful within the field of psychology. Questions of the kind "why do men behave in this way and not differently?" are being substituted by questions of the kind: "how do men behave?" The sciences see themselves obliged to make such a substitution because the notion of "cause" is becoming too fluid in order to be "operative." However, formal explanations are entirely unsatisfactory because they do not reach what interests us existentially. They evade the question: "how may I decide and act within a particular context?" which is the question that provokes every human desire for knowledge.

The above-mentioned thesis, according to which scientific progress is characterized by the progressive decrease of satisfaction of its explanations, comes from the logical analysis of the propositions that compose the scientific discourse. So much so that this is about a "critique of science," and not of all human knowledge. There seems to be therefore, another type of human knowledge that originates from other types of disciplines (for example from philosophy, from artistic intuition, etc.), and which is not reached by the progressive decadence of satisfaction. These would be the types of knowledge for which science is not *competent*. This seems true above all when in relation to an *imperative* knowledge of the kind, "Thou shalt not kill!" This type of knowledge (which would be the source of every ethical and every political action), would be beyond the competence of the sciences, and therefore outside the competence of logical criticism. We may then conclude that although science provides us with explanations that are ever less satisfactory, we dispose of other sources of knowledge that allow us to decide and act despite everything.

However, such an interpretation of the current situation of our knowledge would be erroneous. Science is indeed competent for all of human knowledge, and therefore, *logical criticism is competent for every proposition that formulates any human knowledge*. The discourse of science can be extended over every field of knowledge and can also occupy all of them. In doing so, the discourse turns all of these fields exempt of value and ultimately, exempt of cause. It devalues and removes the cause from all of human knowledge. It manages such a feat as it "translates" the extrascientific propositions into scientific ones. It translates: "Thou shalt not kill!" to: "if you kill, you will be arrested." And it translates: "how beautiful!" to: "this sensation stimulates specific glands." Thus, this devaluation of knowledge does not represent an alternative knowledge, as if we could state: what we have is an ethical and aesthetic knowledge, and even beyond that, scientific knowledge in relation to specific subjects. On the contrary: scientific knowledge blocks knowledge of any other type. As it translates imperative and optative propositions into epistemological propositions, science reveals itself, within the translated propositions, to be made up of defective propositions. The "Thou shalt not kill!" proposition is defective because it is a relation that suppresses one of the sayings ("you will be arrested"). The proposition "how beautiful!" is defective to the point of needing a meaning. Thus science demonstrates that all evaluative knowledge is pseudo-knowledge: *ideology*. And as it unmasks every extrascientific knowledge to be ideological knowledge, science places itself as the *only authority* on matters of knowledge today. So that the above-mentioned logical criticism refers to all of knowledge: all knowledge is becoming progressively less satisfactory.

We may, certainly, rebel against such a scientific imperialism that deprives us of values, but we cannot deny that science is our only authority. What characterizes authority is the fact of being able to dispense with executives in the transmission of its messages: such messages are accepted by consensus. Today, every message emitter (every "power") needs executives, except science. Its messages are accepted by consensus. In a situation where every authority, except science, is "false," it is summarily characteristic that such true authority is so unsatisfactory. So that the critique of science, and the attempts to reformulate science from top-to-bottom, may be interpreted as attempts to *overcome the crisis* in which we find ourselves.

This posits the problem in the relation between science and the critique of science, between *knowledge and wisdom*: in the relation between science and philosophy. One of the aspects that distinguishes our culture in relation to all others is that in the West philosophy gave birth to science, and that science devours the philosophy from which it was born. Wherever science takes hold, from thence philosophy is expelled. For the pre-Socratic Greeks nature was the field of philosophy, and even in the Baroque, as they engaged in natural sciences, they spoke metaphorically of "natural philosophy." Currently, natural phenomena do not allow for philosophizing: science occupies them. The human phenomenon seemed to be philosophy's field for a long time, but it has been occupied by the sciences, above all by psychology, which up until recently was a philosophical discipline, but which currently is a scientific "specialization." The last example of this process is the occupation of the political field by political science, and the field of aesthetics by informatics. *The end of philosophy.* The only remaining field for philosophy now is the field of the critique of science, but this is a slippery field: it slides into science. *Knowledge devours wisdom.*

Hence, here is the current situation of knowledge: we know incomparably more than previous generations. The universe of the discourse of science amplifies itself and grows deeper. Our questions are becoming ever more fertile, and they always provoke new questions. The answers that we are getting from such questions are becoming ever less satisfactory, and the universe is becoming ever more exempt of values and causes. Every extrascientific knowledge is unmasked as ideological and science emancipates us from such ideologies. And our existential questions are revealed to be "bad questions." There is no more room for wisdom, knowledge progresses absurdly.

The universe of the discourse of science, under unlimited expansion, amputates its evaluative and causal dimensions and becomes a formal and empty universe: an existentially meaningless universe. This is verifiable not only by the fact that it is an unimaginable universe, but also that it is a universe that when imagined, is falsified. Science tells us that when we seek to imagine it, we are receiving its messages badly. Thus scientific knowledge refers to a universe that no longer relates to the world in which we live concretely. *Scientific knowledge has become absurd.*

This is the crisis of the sciences that aims to be overcome by phenomenology, as an appeal for us to return to the things in themselves. This crisis has both internal and external aspects that relate to science. But what matters here is the aspect that reveals science to be a *game with symbols.* The scientific universe is a symbolic universe, and its vectors of signification no longer point toward a concrete world, they have been inverted. Scientific "observations" no longer seek to give meaning to symbols, on the contrary, they seek to symbolize the concrete. Today's science is therefore as typical of a post-industrial society as the Newtonian was for the industrial one and the Aristotelian was for the agrarian one. Science has become a game for programmers and a field of functionalism. *Science has become an apparatus.*

Science is an extremely fascinating game, the most entertaining of all games, and the most intelligent of all programs that amuse us. Science diverts our attention above all from the fundamental knowledge that we may know exclusively that which does not interest us. Because everything that interests us, the meaning of life in relation to death, is categorically unknowable since every question that demands such knowledge is a "bad question." And at bottom, that is what we know today: that we can know everything except that which interests us.

OUR HEALTH

Medicine is the biggest scandal of our age. But it is also a starting point for the reformulation of the current crisis in science. Medicine is a hybrid, in which scientific, technical and intuitive elements are badly agglomerated. The reason for this is that the person who is ill is simultaneously *subject* (agent) and *object* (patient), and as object it is extremely complex. The doctor assumes an unbearable position in relation to the patient.

This problem is of an epistemological order. An example: in the Third World the death rate of newborns is becoming lower and in the First World abortion is becoming a free right for all women. Because of this, parents cannot feed their numerous children in the Third World and the few children born in the First World will not be able to feed their retired parents in the future. This shift from the death of newborns to the death of fetuses certainly has economic, social, political and ethical aspects. For example: abortion instead of the death of newborns represents an important step toward women's freedoms. But the important aspect of the problem is epistemological. This transferal means *family programming,* it means social planning. The reasons for programming are functionally irrelevant. It does not matter if the reason for the fight against the death rate of newborns is "noble" (to save lives) or "vile" (to generate cheap manual labor), what counts is that the programming functions imperfectly: it creates new problems. But the program can be perfected. The solution is "zero growth." Abortion and the death rate of newborns must be balanced. The problem is epistemological: *until what point can man and society be objectified and manipulated as an object?*

The problem has two sides. One is that man and society are extraordinarily *complex* objects, so that it is difficult to come to know them. The other side of the problem is that man is a subject that should be *recognized* instead of being known. The first side of the problem asks the question: how can I treat man? The second side asks: how can I assume responsibility for my treatment? The first question is *objective,* the second is *intersubjective.* The doctor sees himself confronted with both questions unable to synthesize them. These are two different epistemological problems.

As an object of knowledge, man may be conceived as being made up of several levels of knowledge. The physical level is more or less quantifiable, and the rest are less quantifiable, as long as they distance themselves from the physical. This is the *internal* problem in science. As subject, man is a being-in-the-world with me ("*Mitsein*"), in which I recognize myself. The more I come to know him, the more I objectify him, the more difficult it becomes for me to recognize myself in him. This is the *external* problem in science, but a problem that puts science as a whole, and as a human activity, into question.

Modern science emerged when craft, as praxis, became dominant in society. The cosmos was no longer experienced as an animate being, but as an extensive space replete of inanimate and animate beings. This suggested a specific *theory of knowledge*; knowledge is the adjustment of the thinking thing to the extended thing. This theory contains *quantification* within its program. The extended thing has a punctual structure: bodies may be decomposed into planes, planes into lines, and lines into points. The thinking thing must therefore posses a structure adjustable to points. It must be composed of clear and distinct elements, of concepts and numbers. The "hard" model of exact knowledge is the adjustment of every concept, every point from the extended thing, into a concept or number. *To know is above all to enumerate.*

This posits the question of the relation between arithmetics and geometry. Arithmetics has a structure that is "empty:" between two numbers, even as close as they may be to each other, there is an interval. Geometry has a structure that is "full:" the points on a line touch each other. If I adjust arithmetics to geometry, an infinite number of points escape through the intervals in between the numbers. The epistemological problem is therefore to close the intervals. Calculus, integrals, and infinitesimals are attempts to close the intervals, but they are not very successful attempts because they also result in clear and distinct concepts, that is, with intervals. For a long time science was able to surpass this difficulty. When it dealt with inanimate things (mechanics, astronomy, inorganic chemistry, electromagnetism etc.) the problem was negligible.

However, when scientific interest established itself over animate things (botanics and zoology), and later over man (psychology, sociology, economy etc.) the problem became a pressing one. It became apparent that animate things may be quantified just like all other things, but that as it was done, something essential escaped through the intervals. Namely: what escaped was the very aspect that distinguishes animate things from inanimate ones. Hence, 19th century science saw itself before an arduous dilemma: to continue quantifying, and thus resign itself to the essential loss of the phenomenon of life, or to elaborate another theory of knowledge and resign itself to the impossibility of quantifying knowledge. 19th century science evaded the dilemma: it divided itself into "hard" sciences (quantifying) and "soft" sciences (non-quantifying). We suffer from this indecision up to this day.

Quantifiable knowledge works technically. The industrial revolution proves that. But such knowledge loses sight of the phenomenon that is alive. The industrial revolution also proves that. Unquantifiable knowledge does not work well technically, or does not even work. The so-called "Science of the Spirit"[3] proves that. Hence the 20th century's attempt to amalgamate the hard and soft sciences. Examples: statistical economy, behavioral psychology, and political science. But such hybrid disciplines are not convincing through the techniques that they apply. The scandal in medicine is a proof of

2 Geisteswissenschaft in the sense applied by Rudolf Steiner. [TN]

46

that. Apparently science is coming up against the *limit of knowledge*. It cannot continue to advance in this direction.

Man, as a subject, posits a problem that is *external* to modern science. The encounter between two subjects is marked by the mutual recognition of one within the other. This *dialogic relation* between subjects is not capable of being incorporated into any theory of modern scientific knowledge. Any theory of knowledge, if it wants to be scientific in the modern sense, presupposes an object to be known, however much it may circumscribe such an object. Hence modern science is *incompetent* for intersubjective encounters. In order to become competent for such encounters, science is obliged to transform the "Other" into an object. This objectification of the subject is possible, and in fact it is done with increasing frequency. There are several methods for objectification available: violence, persuasion, and the subtle manipulation of the subject. Once the objectification is done, science becomes competent for intersubjective encounters; the "social sciences" become possible. However, the price paid for the extension of scientific competence to include man and society is high. Dialogue is sacrificed, and with it recognition is sacrificed in favor of knowledge. The result is the *solitude* of knowledge: a knowledge that is neither recognized nor recognizable. Thus, if knowledge is not recognized dialogically, if it is not the result of dialogue, and if it does not aim toward the Other, it becomes absurd. As science objectifies man and society, the knowledge that it produces becomes absurd. And this problematizes science as a whole, as a human enterprise. The current tendency toward the objectification of man in science is a suicidal tendency. It transforms science into an inhuman apparatus.

Medicine is, therefore, the preferential discipline for illustrating both problems of knowledge. It illustrates not only the limits of quantifiable knowledge, but also the fundamental absurdity of an objectifying knowledge of man. The *scandal of medicine* is not so much the situation in the hospitals and asylums, not even the flagrant injustice of social medicine, above all in the Third World, but precisely the epistemological viscosity of medicine. However, precisely because the factors of the crisis of science collide more clearly within medicine, it could represent one of the points from which an attempt to overcome the crisis may begin. The doctor's position before the patient is so untenable that he sees himself obliged to seek another position, for *a new scientific attitude*. The doctor sees himself obliged to change attitude, not because of a consideration for the theory of knowledge, but because of the problematic derived from his own praxis, which in turn, is the application of the theory of a knowledge in crisis. The crisis of modern science manifests itself in the doctor as a conflict of conscience, and is thus interiorized.

The *civil engineer* knows just as well as the surgeon about the current crisis of knowledge. He knows that the precision with which he calculates the bridge is a problem. And he knows that the bridge will have effects upon the situation that are not quantifiable: aesthetic effects, for example. He knows even that the bridge will change the life of men. But as a functionary of the roads construction apparatus he does not see himself obliged to assume the responsibility of such problems. His competence is only to build bridges. The surgeon is in a different position. The precision with which he operates with the skeleton is comparable to the operation with steel on the bridge, the effects that the operation will have are equally incalculable, and the operation will equally change a human life. But the doctor cannot avoid the responsibility as the engineer can: whether he likes it or not, the surgeon recognizes himself in the patient.

The *political scientist* knows as well as the psychiatrist about the current crisis of knowledge. He knows of the imprecision of the scenarios that he is projecting, of the "softness" of the models that he employs, and he knows that he manipulates and objectifies society. But as a functionary of the administrative apparatus, he does not see himself obliged to assume the responsibility of such problems. His responsibility is limited to the "margins of error" of his projects. The psychiatrist is in a different position. The imprecision, the "softness" of the models that he employs is comparable to the models of political science, but the psychiatrist recognizes himself in the patient onto whom he applies such models. Thus the civil engineer and the political scientist are conscious of the epistemological problem, while the surgeon and the psychiatrist experience it through praxis. They must decide: they either abandon the objectification of man and sacrifice scientific technique, or they abandon the attempts to assume existential responsibility for their treatment – an impossible choice.

The solution for the impasse lies in a change of attitude in relation to knowledge. *Knowledge must be admitted as being one among the different forms of human existence.* A form that is inseparable from the others, under the pain of becoming inhuman. Man is in the world to experience it, evaluate it, and know it. He can only know what he experiences and evaluates. A science that does not admit to this, that does not admit to its aesthetic and political dimensions, is an inhuman science. Only after science has assumed such responsibilities, will it begin to elaborate theories of knowledge. With effect: there are symptoms of this reformulation of scientific attitude, and of new theories of knowledge. Above all in the phenomenological attitude, which no longer presupposes that knowledge is necessarily objectifying. But until the scientific revolution reformulates modern science as a whole, our health will continue to be that of surviving, but undernourished children, and that of aborted fetuses.

OUR COMMUNICATION

The previous essay made the distinction between two types of knowledge: the *objective* and the *intersubjective*. The first speaks of objects; it is *discursive*. The second speaks with Others; it is *dialogic*. In the case of medicine: the doctor speaks objectively about the illness and dialogues intersubjectively with the patient. What distinguishes discourse from dialogue is above all the climate: dialogue happens in a climate of responsibility. *Responsibility is openness for answers*. There are already symptoms that point to a reformulation of science from discourse into dialogue. In the case of medicine, psychoanalysis is an example. In order to grasp the impact of such a reformulation it is necessary for us to look at the structure of human communication.

Man has the capacity to store acquired experiences, and to transmit them. That is: man is a historical being. In other terms: man produces, stores, and transmits new information. He increases the sum of available information. That is what history is. This contradicts the second principle of thermodynamics, which affirms the progressive decrease of the sum of all information within a closed system (the world). *History,* as a dam for new information, *is antinatural.* This obviously does not justify the dichotomous distinction between nature and culture, between "spirit" and "matter." History does not invalidate the laws of nature. These are still valid for culture: the information accumulated in the course of history will end up *forgotten.* Papers covered with symbols will turn into dust, cities will crumble, and entire civilizations will disappear without a trace. However, this justifies the dialectic distinction between nature and culture. Human communication opposes itself dialectically to the natural tendency toward entropy. History is a negatively entropic epicycle that superimposes itself over nature's tendency; its antithesis.

Hence, communication has two different aspects: the *productive* aspect of information and the cumulative aspect. The production of information is not an "*ex nihilo*" creation: new information is produced through the synthesis of available information. Such a synthetic method is called "dialogue." The accumulation of information happens due to the transmission of information toward memories (human or other), in which the information is deposited. Such a distributive method is called "discourse." Every discourse presupposes dialogue, because it presupposes dialogically elaborated information. Every dialogue presupposes discourse, because it presupposes the reception of information to be synthesized. Human society reveals itself thus as a communicative fabric in which such discourses and dialogues are dynamically integrated. This is the dynamic of history. Whenever one of these two methods of communication prevails over the other, society finds itself in danger; it demands an always-precarious balance between dialogue and discourse.

Western society is a very specific communicative fabric. It is not only characterized by the communicated *topics,* but above all by the *methods* through which it communicates them. Generally speaking, the West elaborated two types of dialogue and four types of discourse. Dialogues are *circular* (examples: round tables, paliaments) and *networked* (examples: the telephone system, public opinion). Discourses are *theatric* (examples: lectures, concerts), *pyramidal* (examples: armies, churches), *trees* (examples: sciences, arts), and *amphitheatric* (examples: radio, press). Western history may be seen as a communicative game that applies such communicative methods as strategies. The aim of all of these strategies is to produce and accumulate new information.

Western society's current situation is marked by the predominance of discourses over dialogues. The general complaint of "lack of communication" has been badly formulated. The loneliness within the mass, which is the basis of the complaint, is not a consequence of the poverty of the communicative fabric. On the contrary: never before have Western discourses worked so well as they do now, and above all never before have the tree of science and the amphitheater of mass communication worked so well. The solitude within the mass is a consequence of our growing difficulty to enter into dialogic communication with others. Under the daily bombardment of extremely well distributed discourses we all dispose of the same information, and every dialogic exchange of information is becoming redundant. Our feeling of loneliness is due to our growing incapacity to elaborate new information in dialogue with others. Under the *domain of the discourses, the social fabric of the West decomposes itself.* It urges us, therefore, to analyze such discourses.

The *theatric* discourse is the oldest and antecedes history. This is the patriarchal discourse that transmits the tribal myths to a new generation; it is the grandmother's discourse that tells the legends to the grandchildren. That which characterizes this type of discourse is the fact that the receivers face the emitter: they form a semi-circle around him. They are in a position to challenge him with questions, and he is in a position of responsibility: he is obliged to answer. Theater is a discourse that is open for dialogues. The challenge, the turning of discourse into dialogue, the "revolution," is within the theater's program. Revolutions are possible around the bonfire or the fireplace.

From the late Neolithic, this becomes a disadvantage. When it involves collective enterprises such as the building of channels and cities, what is intended is not dialogue, but obedience. Society must be able to hear the messages but without being able to challenge them. In order to achieve this method of discourse, it is necessary that the emitter becomes inaccessible to the receivers. This is the *pyramidal* method of discourse that is to be introduced; the one that will become the communicational basis of Western history. It consists of the introduction of hierarchically organized *relays* between the emitter and the receivers. The first example of the pyramid is the ecclesiastic realm. Within it the messages start from an inaccessible "author" (a god), and pass through "authorities," *relays* whose function is to keep such messages "pure" of noise, and of barring access to the emitter for the receivers. The climate of responsibility, prevalent in the theater, is substituted for the climate of tradition and of religiosity. Tradition because the *relays* tra-dict,[4] and "religion" because they re-link the receivers to the author of the message. Thus, the climate of the late Neolithic continues to characterize current pyramids, such as the Church, State, army, political parties and companies.

The disadvantage of this communicative strategy is that dialogue becomes difficult. This strategy is good for the storage of information but bad for the elaboration of new information – the social fabric stagnates. Hence the reforms that the pyramid underwent during the Renaissance; the aim was to preserve the efficiency of the pyramid and simultaneously open it up for dialogue. The *relays* were transformed into dialogic circles, but conserved their organization as a hierarchy. The result was the *tree discourse*. That is the characteristic discourse of modernity. The substitution of authorities for dialogic circles subdivided the pyramidal discourse into branches (specialisms) that tended to sub-ramify and to crisscross. This restructuring revealed itself to be extremely fertile. Every branch of the discourse started to progressively produce more new

---

4 Flusser does a play with words in Portuguese, which is difficult to approximate – he plays with the word "tradição" and from it forms "tra-dizem," by playing with the concept of "dicção" or "diction" which comes from "dictio" in Latin and which means to express, but which is not contained within the root of the word "tradition" in English. In this case Flusser is playing more with the phonetic character of the word in order to extract a different meaning. Thus by "tra-dicting," one could say that the relays perpetuate the same expression without altering it. [TN]

information. The dynamic of the tree discourse flooded society with a real cascade of new information. However, there was an unexpected consequence. Every dialogic circle elaborated a specific code in which the new information was synthesized. The information thus codified became decipherable only for the "specialists" (the participants of the branch). Hence the messages of the tree discourse tended to be indecipherable for society as a whole, which "re-clericized" and "re-authorized" the discourse. The "laymen" no longer grasped the messages that came from different trees: neither the ones from nuclear physics or microbiology, nor the ones from advanced techniques or avant-garde art. So that from the 20th century onwards the tree discourses stopped having a general reception and became absurd as communicative methods.

The solution of the problem is to translate the messages from the tree discourses into socially decipherable codes: to build apparatus that "transcode." The result of this is the *amphitheatric discourse*. This is what characterizes current times. The mass communication apparatus are black-boxes that transcode the messages from the trees of science, of technique, of art, of political science, into extremely simple and poor codes. Thus transcoded, the messages are irradiated toward a space and whoever floats within such a space, if synchronized, tuned and programmed for such, will receive the irradiated messages. "Mass culture" is the result of this method of discursive communication. The transcoding and irradiation of messages results in the transformation of the original structure: the trees work linearly, the *media,* multidimensionally. If we admit that linearity is the structure of history, then *media* present themselves as post-historical communication. They are black-boxes that have history as *input* and post-history as *output*. They are programmed to transcode history into post-history, events into programs.

In the current situation, the four types of discourse co-exist. But the theatric discourses (schools, theaters, etc.), and the pyramidal discourses (State, party, etc.), are in crisis; they are communicational anachronisms that are difficult to assimilate into the dominant communicational fabric. The most obvious example of the problem is the family, which is a pyramid and theater. The tree discourses continue to ramify and are coupled to the amphitheatric discourses that transcode the messages. *Thus mass media are becoming the preferential source of available information.* They are the ones that codify our world. We live in a post-historical climate.

Theatric discourse programs *circular dialogues.* The pyramidal discourse seeks to exclude dialogue of any type. The tree discourse programs the circular dialogues for specialists. The amphitheatric discourse programs *networked dialogues.* The theater demands that the message be dialogued in order to produce new information. The pyramid forbids dialogue. The tree demands a specific, elitist competence in order to be able to participate in the elaboration of new information. The amphitheater demands that the irradiated information be transformed dialogically into an amorphous soup, into "public opinion," in order to serve as feedback for the emitting apparatus. The aim of networked dialogues is not the production of new information but feedback. The apparatus have elaborated specific methods (public census, marketing, public opinion research, public elections, etc.) in order to receive the feedback. "Democracy," in the sense of a dialogue that produces information that is not elitist, is only possible within the theater. In the situation of current democracy, it is impossible. The feeling of loneliness in the masses is a consequence of this. *Democracy is not in the program.*

Therefore, to reformulate science dialogically, implies a reformulation of society's communicational fabric; to democratize it. But such an epistemological task is thus a *political task*. It is a case of making science politically responsible. To transform into method the awareness that knowledge is only meaningful if it is a starting point for republican action. However, so that such reformulation may be done it is necessary for a republic to exist. And the republic is the public space for circular dialogues. Currently such a space does not exist. Every space is occupied by the amphitheatric irradiations and by networked dialogue. If seen internally, the crisis of science presents itself as an epistemological crisis, but if seen from the point of view of society, it is a structural crisis: it is not possible to dialogize knowledge if there is no space for it. The discursive and dialogically elitist character of science owes itself structurally to its coupling with channels of mass communication. In order to bring about a new theory of intersubjective knowledge it is necessary to dispose of a space for intersubjectivity. The current crisis of science must therefore be seen from within the context of the current communicational situation. As long as there is no space for politics and for non-elitist circular dialogues, the crisis of science is insoluble.

OUR RHYTHM

The apparatus that program us are synchronized. For example: the transport apparatus is synchronized with the industrial apparatus, and the administrative apparatus with the entertainment one. This synchronicity is the rhythm that marks our lives. This essay proposes to consider the functionality of rhythm within a significant example.

In the classic city the *basilica* had a decisive role, and under a different form, it continues to function in our current situation, although radically transcoded. The basilica is an empty space covered by a dome. The example of the Roman Pantheon illustrates its use. In the beginning it was used as a market, that is: a public space dedicated to the exchange of goods and ideas; a dialogic space. Later it was transformed into a temple, that is: a space dedicated to the contemplation of idols, of immutable ideas; a theoretical space. Later still, it was transformed into a church, that is: a space dedicated to contemplation in the Christian sense of the term. The basilica had thus two successive functions: the political and the theoretical. In our current situation, both functions of the basilica have been recoded, although its structure as a space covered by a dome has been preserved. It has become the *supermarket*, which simulates the political space and the *cinema*, which simulates the theoretical space, and both are synchronized.

The supermarket is a labyrinth made up of messages coded into images (colorful conserves, bottles, labels, posters), and sounds (irradiated by loud-speakers). The labyrinth swallows-up the message receivers. It has widely open entrances in order to create the illusion of a public space, of an "agora" in a "polis," as if the supermarket was a place of exchanges, of dialogues and evaluation of values. In reality, every dialogue is made impossible by the constant bombardment of colorful and audible messages that fill the space discursively. The supermarket is a fraudulent republic.

But it is fraudulent, above all, for being a trap. It does not have free exits. Whoever wishes to escape is obliged to queue at the narrow slots that serve as exits, and to pay a ransom. The supermarket is a prison, the most private of all spaces. It does not serve for dialogic exchanges, but imposes discursively, imperatively, a specific behavior of consumption upon the receivers of its messages. And the method it employs is that of seduction, a method that is characteristic of the objectification of man by apparatus. *The supermarket is an apparatus that simulates the republic in order to seduce its receivers so that they may be manipulated as consuming objects.*

The cinema is the opposite side of the supermarket. Its entrance is the narrow opening that obliges those who wish to participate in its mysteries to queue. These queues are the counterpart of the ones that form in the supermarket. And the *obolus* that the future receiver of the filmic message sacrifices at the entrance is the opposite of the coin he sacrifices at the supermarket exit. But at least the cinema opens its doors widely once its program has ended. These exit doors are the counterparts of the supermarket's entrance doors. The newly programmed mass of viewers flows, amorphously, from the exits in order to pulverize itself into individual particles (mass men), and to re-crystallize itself in the form of queues at the supermarkets' exit. Between the supermarkets' and the cinemas' queues there are other channels, for example busses and urban trains that form and inform the mass. It is within these synchronized channels that our lives pulsate.

The cinema is a basilica without windows, a cave. It is the black uterus, the Great Mother that generates and devours. Within it shadows appear. The Platonic myth of the cave describes it, and Plato could be considered as the first film critic. Before the shadows appear on the screen, the darkness and silence of the cinema reigns. Thus the cinema creates the illusion of being a contemplative space, dedicated to "theory" (from "theorein" – to contemplate). The cinema creates the illusion of being a theater. But this is a fraud. The cinema is not a theatric structure: in it there is no stage from which the emitter confronts the receiver. In the cinema there is an apparatus that projects the messages from an absent emitter. In reality the cinema is one among the many transmitters of an amphitheatric apparatus: the cinema industry. It is one of the antennae of a discourse whose center is beyond the receivers' horizon.

61

The illusion that the cinema is a theater is provoked at its entrance; where there are light and sound messages emitted that seduce the gullible to contemplate the program. However, it is characteristic of the cinema that such light messages blink. They are in collusion with future viewers. When they enter the cave, they find themselves in a geometrically organized space (chairs, "extended things," that form rows) and arithmetically ordered (the chairs are numbered). But as the viewers occupy the seats, it is not a case of a Cartesian adjustment of thinking things to extended things, because the seated viewers become themselves the extended things as they allow the gigantic shadows on the screen and the sound vibrations to fill the space and manipulate them. The cinema perpetrates the miracle of transubstantiation from thinking things into extended things. And in this sense it effectively continues to be a church.

Over the heads of the faithful and from behind their backs, works a film projector. It is an apparatus programmed to project images ordered on a filmstrip onto the screen, so as to create the illusion of movement. The receivers are conscious of the optical fraud of which they are victims, since they know more or less the function of the apparatus. They have miniatures at home. Notwithstanding, if they turn their heads in the direction of the projector, it is not in order to liberate themselves from the illusion, but in anger if the apparatus malfunctions and the shadows jump instead of moving smoothly. They become angry if the illusion is unmasked.

This behavior, contrary to the platonic prisoners is surprising. How can the manipulated collaborate to such a high degree with the apparatus that transform them into objects? How can they collaborate to such a high degree to their own annihilation as subjects? It is the same question, however mitigated, that is present in Auschwitz. And here, as well as there, reasonable answers are not short. The viewers know that the projection apparatus is not the emitter of the fraudulent message, but only the last link in a chain that connects it to the inaccessible emitter. It would therefore be irrational to wish to rebel against the projector and to want to destroy it. Neither would it be reasonable to wish to burn the filmstrip that unravels within it. They are only copies of inaccessible prototypes. The fraudulent message cannot be eliminated at the cinema by viewers, no matter how many. If the whole cinema were destroyed, the fraudulent message would continue to be transmitted untouched in several cinemas of the same type. The amphitheatric apparatus, of which the cinema is an antenna, would remain undamaged. The viewers know therefore that the cinema is a space that excludes every revolutionary action and behave accordingly.

However, such a reasonable explanation of this surprising behavior is not good. It is not true that the viewers do not rebel because they cannot. The truth is that they do not rebel because they do not want to. Their behavior proves that they *want to be deceived*. With effect: this desire to be deceived is the consensus of mass society. If such a consensus did not exist, then the apparatus-like totalitarianism that is readying would not be comprehensible. And this implies that every effort, individual or collective, toward the emancipation of society from the deception exerted by the apparatus that program it, as well as every effort toward the demystification of the world codified by apparatus, be it as understood by a "Kulturkritik," be it differently, will come across such a consensus; but paradoxically, because every effort toward the "democratization of society" is deeply antidemocratic, in the sense of being aimed against the will of the vast majority.

But it is necessary to consider this consensus closely. The will to be deceived, the will to be victims of fraud, is the exact opposite of religious faith. The viewers at the cinema occupy, in relation to the shadows that move on the screen, an opposite position as occupied by the viewers of the Malaysian shadow theater. They know perfectly well that the shadows are illusory, but they believe in such an illusion despite their knowledge of it. They believe in the shadows out of "bad faith," deliberately. The cinema works, for them, as deliberate second-degree magic, as artificial magic. The myths that the cinema projects are myths deliberately programmed and received in conscience of such myth-making deliberation. It is therefore not correct to state that the cinema is an alienating instrument. The cinema, as all of our *media*, produces myths thanks to a conscious collusion between the emitters and receivers of its messages. There is nothing to de-mystify in this case.

The supermarket and the cinema form the two wings of a fan that instigates in the mass the movement of progress. In the cinema the mass is programmed for consumer behavior at the supermarket, and from the supermarket the mass is freed to re-program itself at the cinema. This circulation between supermarket and cinema is an aspect of the metabolism of the mass, which is far too complex in its totality in order to be explained, unless cybernetically. Mass culture is only explainable through its *input* and *output*, through the *programs* that are fed into it and the behavior that results from this. The cinematographic programs are the "old story that is always new." They are always repetitive variations of the same themes. Because they are post-historical re-codifications of history, which serve them as a pretext: they play with the elements of history, *they are games*. Films are the result of a game with history, played out within the black-boxes of the cinematographic apparatus that seek to program the masses. And the supermarkets are the places where such programs become behavior. Which means that the rhythm of mass society is the manifestation of "the eternal recurrence of the same as will to power" in an anti-Nietzschean sense.

The programmers of these programs, the producers of films and of supermarkets, are players. They interfere with events *from the outside*, in the case of producers, with glue and splicer. They transcend history and play with it. They live trans-historically. History is for them an object. However, simultaneously, they also function as a function of the programs that they program. They are programmed to program. This is made manifest in their behavior. They also oscillate between cinema and supermarket. *In mass society there is no elite, only specialists.* We are all pieces in a game, inside which we oscillate rhythmically.

The supermarket and the cinema are wings of just one of the many fans that blow on us, of just one of the many windmills that turn over our heads. This turning, which is gradually more autonomous, grinds us all into amorphous flour. Every attempt to rebel against the windmills is Quixotic. The only hope in such a situation is to become conscious of the absurd stupidity of the automatic rotation that propels us. The awareness of the fact that behind the rotation, nothing "hides," literally. That it is the absurd rotation that is the reality of apparatus. With such awareness we may at least be propelled centrifugally out of functionalism toward nothingness.

OUR DWELLING

A profound change in the way we dwell is underway. A change comparable only to the one at the beginning of the Neolithic, when we became sedentary. We are abandoning the sedentary way of life. We are on the move, as individuals and groups. A distant observer will have the image of an anthill that has been disturbed by a transcendental foot.

In this, it cannot be a case of a return to nomadism. Gypsies are not on the move; they are rooted in the tribe. To dwell does not mean to sleep in a fixed bed, but to live in a *habitual setting*. The home is not a fixed place, but a place of support that deserves trust. To have lost a home does not mean to have abandoned a place, but to have to live in a non-habitual place, therefore uninhabitable. Or to have to live in a place where we do not recognize ourselves. We are on the move, because our world has been so radically transformed that it has become unhabitual and uninhabitable. We do not recognize ourselves in it. And we cannot habituate ourselves to that.

The habitual is imperceptible. Habit is an opaque covering that conceals the environment. Within our home-landscape, we only perceive events and not the foundational structures. If the foundational structures are currently that which is shocking for us in the environment, then it is because there has been a structural transformation. The recodification of our world by apparatus has made our world strange to us. We are uprooted, because the ground in which our roots rest has suffered a tectonic tremor. This allows us to assume a distanced and critical position in relation to our world. The world has become strange, it no longer deserves trust, and as foreigners in the world we may critique it. But as Kant used to say, critique or doubt, is not a dwelling. *The reason for our critique is the longing we feel.* Due to our radical alienation, we are reactionaries, anti-reformists: we no longer dwell.

The transcoding of our world by apparatus has provoked the *migration of peoples*. We are all on the move. It is not only the Hindus in London that have lost their homeland: Londoners have also lost theirs. And it is not only the *Nordestinos* that have lost theirs in São Paulo: *Paulistanos* have also lost theirs. That is because London and São Paulo have become unhabitual and uninhabitable. The current migration of peoples has shuffled history and geography. The Hindus' mystical time and the *Nordestinos*' magical time, have become synchronized with the Londoners' and the *Paulistanos*' historical time. We are experiencing São Paulo and London with a kind of quad-dimensionality of shuffled space-time. Historical categories are not enough in order for us to grasp this. And this is turning such cities unhabitual and uninhabitable. We no longer recognize in them the products of our history and therefore no longer recognize ourselves in them.

This migration of peoples is constituted of successive waves of barbarians that invade the scene from the horizon. But this time it does not come from the steppe. They sprout from the open uteruses of undernourished young women, these matriarchs of the future. If we contemplate the suffered faces of these young women of color, we recognize in them the triple rape of which they are victims; by their own men, by the society in which we take part, and by apparatus. We recognize thus in such a face, our own past: our own crimes. *The face of the future has traces of our past.* And that is the real reason why we, the "bourgeois," are on the move. We are running away from our past. Our past chases us. The waves of babies with sick bellies that spring from the uteruses of the young women of color propel us toward progress.

This situation is unhabitual: *that we have the future at our backs.* That nowadays "to progress" does not mean to demand the future, but to avoid the past. That, in the case of an apparatus-like progress, it is no longer the case of opening up the field for the future, but to "resolve" the problems created by the past in the form of starving babies. That our progress, is a method to avoid being devoured by the past that chases us. This is unhabitual: that *progress has become a form of reaction.* That we are reactionaries precisely for being progressives.

However, it is not this that makes the migration of peoples so terrifying. The terror is the fact that "humanity," the starving babies, advances in the same direction, toward which we are escaping. That future humanity seeks to reach and overtake us. That everyone, fugitives and chasers, are being sucked toward the same programming abyss of apparatus. That the whole of humanity, "old" and "new," is "developing" according to a program.

Within such general development it is necessary to distinguish between three types of superimposed motion: the short-term, the mid-term, and the long-term. The motion of the sea may serve as a model. The short-term motion is the waves that end on the beach. The mid-term, the tides and the long-term are the changes that the sea provokes on the shores of the continent. If we wish to grasp the dynamics of the current migration of peoples, we must distinguish it in terms of these levels, at the risk of turning such migration even more tragic.

The *short-term* motion manifests itself, in the First World, as the traffic jams on the motorways in search of snow in December, or in search of sunshine in July. In the Third World, it manifests itself as the overloaded trucks that follow the harvest of monocultures. The *mid-term* motion manifests itself, in the First World, as social mobility (the rise of the proletariat and the decadence of the bourgeoisie). In the Third World it manifests itself as the monstrous swelling of the cities. The *long-term* motion manifests itself, in the world as a whole, as the inexorable advancement of the tropical population toward temperate climate, as in the "developed" world, by the inexorable advancement from the "south" toward the "north." The long-term manifests itself as the invasion of the historical, apparatus-like societies by the "pre-historic" ones, which seek to "conquer history," but which in reality advance into post-history.

One example of the danger of the confusion between such levels can be given in the case of *urban planning*. The urban planners currently seek to channel the mid-term migration. The French *"villes neuves"* seek to build "homes" for the African immigrants, and the "dismantling of the favelas" seek to absorb the *Nordestinos* within the para-Western cities of the south of Brazil. Their projects envisage twenty years, which is how long such "homes" last. But as they do it, the urban planners are overflowing the mid-term. They are penetrating the long-term with their projects, which is not as long as they think. The starving babies will not stay for such a long time in the projected homes. Their patience is not so long. They will use these urban projects as a temporary area. They will move from the dismantled favelas into Brasília and from the *"villes neuves"* into the historic city-centers before the time predicted. The future is at our heels and will catch up with us before the time predicted in our projects. We are myopic programmers: we do not grasp the essence of the migration of peoples.

This myopia of our programs is comprehensible. It seems that the current migration can in fact be channeled in the mid-term, since phenomena such as starving babies in Grenoble is nothing new. For example: the Sudeten in Bavaria after the Second World War, the Pied Noirs in Marseille after the Algerian war, the Khmers and the Cubans in Florida right now. But the babies in Grenoble are a different phenomenon. They are not refugees, they are invaders. The Hindus are invading London, the Turks Hamburg, the *Nordestinos* São Paulo and the Algerians Grenoble. Our programmers are not aware of this because the babies do not behave like invaders. The Hindus do not arrive in London as the Londoners once arrived in Delhi. They are not occupying palaces but slums. This is because the invaders are not winners. In the current migration of peoples such a category does not exist: they are all defeated. They are all "undergoing development." The invaders are undergoing development faster than us, they are catching up and they are going to overtake us in order to be defeated faster, better programmed. This is the long-term tendency of the migration of peoples.

The invasion of the First World by the Third World is unhabitual in several aspects: for example, by the fact that the invaders are babies. That is why we do not have models at our disposal in order to grasp the event. Instead of elaborating myopic and hypocritical strategies in order to channel the phenomenon (for example, "developmental aid"), it urges us to elaborate models that allow us to grasp it. And curiously, such models are available in unexpected places. *Aesthetics* provides models to grasp unhabitual and unusual phenomena. It is useful to apply them to the phenomenon of the migration of peoples.

The habitual is perceived as the experienced. The habitual is experienced as the *beautiful*. That is the basis for patriotism. The homeland is more beautiful than any other landscape simply for passing unnoticed. Patriotism is kitsch. The unhabitual is perceived and experienced as terrifying. It is *ugly*. Starving babies in Grenoble are ugly. Between the habitual and the unhabitual, the beautiful and the ugly, there is a tension that can be overcome by a leap. The leap is experienced as *beauty*. Beauty is the experience of overcoming terror. The history of art is

72

cyclical: beautiful-ugly-pretty-beautiful. Because beauty becomes prettiness when it is habituated.

The leap from ugliness toward prettiness is an arduous process. The Cubists learned the hard way to leap from African ugliness toward the beauty of the Rive Gauche and the receivers of their message learned the hard way to follow the leap. Currently, every young woman from a respectable family paints like the Cubists. Those that eat pizza find it ugly to eat monkeys' hands, but they should learn the hard way that it is a delicious dish. Currently the supermarkets sell monkeys' hands as conserves. The transformation of terror into beauty demands effort. The transformation of beauty into kitsch happens spontaneously.

This aesthetic model is applicable to the current migration of peoples. We should learn to discover the beauty in the terror of the event: to discover the beauty in the starving babies and the suffering young women of color. To speak archaically: we should learn to love them. And as "love" is recognition in the Other, we should learn to recognize ourselves in the future that chases us, which is our past. We should, in other words, learn to love the future that is no longer ours. And we should do it in full knowledge that this future envisages the programming that will devour us.

However this is not a supra-human task ("Christian" for example). It has always been accomplished everywhere. Everyone, when they get old, lives in an unhabitual and uninhabitable environment: in the world of their grandchildren. We should love the future, the starving babies, as our grandchildren. Of which Goethe refers to as the fiercest of beasts. In other words: we should admit that our world is dying and we should love that. We should not expect anything for ourselves from this engagement in favor of such a hostile future. It must be a pure engagement. If we apprehend such high art, such "*ars moriendi,*" then the terror of current times will become an "adventure:" the experience of the beautiful. And, curiously, we may thus live again. Because openness to death is the real dwelling of man: he who exists for death. In the current migration of peoples, we have the privilege to be able to experience openness to death not only as individuals but also collectively. We are experiencing our openness to the death of our culture.

Our Shrinking

The 19th century and the first half of the 20th century are characterized by gigantism; machines, cities, empires, profits, sporting records, discoveries, expectations. In sum, everything grew, swelled and reached monstrous proportions. This tendency is still valid, above all in the Third World. But since the Second World War, the opposite tendency also makes itself manifest, a tendency toward the pigmy, the dwarf, and the miniature. Mottos such as, "think small," "small is beautiful," and "less is more" start to compete with the grandiloquent discourses, above all in the First World. An "alternative" counter-revolution is under way, and it is the opposite of the industrial and technical revolution. So that currently, we are able to note the two principle symptoms of senility: *we swell-up and shrink, simultaneously.*

The shrinking started within the field of *physics*. The Newtonian model of an infinite and eternal universe was substituted by the model of a finite universe made up of wrinkles with wrinkles, with little wrinkles. Research was focused on the most ephemeral and smallest particles and the term "atom" acquired a dominant and menacing meaning. Therefore it became obvious that the minimal exerts a fascination that is in no way inferior to the enormous. This experience spread on to other fields. Within *politics* it made real the awareness that in order to modify the fabric of society, it is not necessary to have gigantic institutions such as the State, classes and parties in sight. Because what is more decisive is the modification of the smaller elements of society, such as the family, marriage, sexual behavior, and units of work – and small action groups (terrorists and others) that start to occupy one of the central spotlights of the scene. Within *economy* there emerged, next to the gigantic multinationals and the international syndicates, miniature units of the type "do it yourself," "ecological" cooperatives and kibbutzim. Within *art,* tendencies toward "minimal art," ephemeral "happenings" and dodecaphonic mini-compositions, started to compete with the colossal "shows" of the mass entertainment apparatus. Within *religion*, small and quite often violent sects opposed themselves to the gigantic apparatus of the established religions. All of these tendencies toward the minimal pretend to propose *alternatives to the megalomania of apparatus.* What this pretention is worth may be evaluated if we take into consideration this tendency within the field of technology. Because it is within this field that miniatures are better, more concretely graspable.

Intelligent instruments are instruments that are equipped with mini-memory and mini-program that execute specific tasks automatically. They cook dinners, cut grass, write letters, and assemble cars. They are robots in every sense; *they are not anthropomorphic*, to the contrary as predicted by all the preceding science fiction. Because these miniatures, far from being anti-apparatus, are themselves apparatus; and they work within and in function of gigantic apparatus. Therefore the de-alienating pretention of the defenders of miniaturization seems doubtful.

These instruments are rapidly becoming smaller, cheaper, numerous and more intelligent. They flow from industry to public and private administration and from there to the living room and the kitchen. Wherever they install themselves, they transform the environment into an apparatus. Robots that cut dresses, transform the tailors' shops into apparatus and "word processors" transform offices into apparatus. Intelligent kitchens transform the home into a chemistry laboratory and miniature TVs transform the pockets of suits into sophisticated apparatus. If we imagine a garage completely decked out with intelligent apparatus, as the cars there already are, we will have imagined the *post-industrial society*: a society fully equipped with apparatus.

Microchips are the guiding principle of miniaturization.[5] They are silicone "chips" that allow for the storage of a large quantity of information into a very small space. This *industrial counter-revolution* will modify man just as much as the Industrial Revolution did. *Anthropologically* speaking, this is a case of transferal of models in relation to such counter-revolution. Before the Industrial Revolution,

---

5 In the original Flusser uses the term semiconductors to describe what we generally refer today as microchips. Semiconductor devices are the different electronic parts of an integrated circuit, such as diodes and transistors, which as a circuit can also be referred as chip or microchip and the most advanced integrated circuits are the microprocessors that control all of our contemporary digital apparatus. [TN]

models were in the "head" of the craftsman. After the revolution, they became stored in the tool. Thanks to the counter-revolution they have become stored in the programs of intelligent instruments. Therefore such instruments provide the models for individual producers, who are thus capacitated to produce consumer goods at home.

This transferal of models implies a radical modification of human life. In pre-industrial society, models are *ideals*. The shoemaker has the image of the ideal shoe in his head and seeks to force the leather to adapt to the image. His aim is to produce the ideal shoe. This characterizes the philosophy and religion of Antiquity and of the Middle Ages: from Plato to Thomas Aquinas models were considered as immutable ideals that "revealed" themselves to the theoretical gaze and to faith. In industrial society, models are improvable *forms*. The engineers and designers have progressively improved the tool of the industrial shoe. That is characteristic of the philosophy of the Modern Age. From Kant to Marx and Nietzsche, the central problem of philosophy was the manipulability of models. "To know" was to adapt the models to the phenomenon to be known. Theoretical science elaborated models increasingly better adapted. And the central question in modern politics was: "who should own the means of production that elaborate and apply models to cultural goods?"

The counter-revolution of "chips" transforms models into *information*. The intelligent instruments contain the models as programmed information. Thus the problematic of modern philosophy, of science and politics, is gradually surpassed. The interest becomes diverted to logical and structural questions. Philosophy stops being "critical" and becomes "analytical." In science models become computable calculations. In politics it is no longer a case of the critique of culture and of "power," and it becomes a case of the analysis of the functionality of society's programs.

The radical change provoked by the transformation of models becomes more evident in the arts. In Modern Art it was a case of the elaboration of new models. That which was sought was "originality" and every new model was taken as an improvement: "*avant garde* art." Currently, that which is sought is a maximum of information, reached by the equilibrium between "noise" and "redundancy." The artistic activity is seen as informative and in this sense modeling. In sum: *the counter-revolution of "chips" gradually abolishes modern life*, and gradually creates a new type of life that is unimaginable for now.

In the program of the intelligent instruments, models are neither immutable ideals, nor improvable forms. They are tiny "imprints." Models no longer come from the transcendental (from the Realm of Ideas, from God), nor are they "inventions" of genial men (technicians, scientists, politicians, philosophers, artists). They are the result of minute combinations of "bits" done by programmers, system analysts and other similar anonymous functionaries. Such models evoke neither divine images nor visions inspired by *mosaics*. Or even better, they evoke *ideograms* that work. Such models have an unsophisticated Oriental character.

Is it not the case that the counter-revolution of "chips" processes itself in Japan faster than elsewhere, and that China emerges as the most adequate society for the miniaturization of production and consumption? Suffice to see the shoeless doctors, the high ovens in the backyards and the portable kitchens. Suffice to see the miniaturized trees and cockerels. The counter-revolution of "chips" has a *Confucian* character. It seeks to transform society into a mosaic with its ideographic programs, to be programmed by strategies of the game "go." It seeks to transform man into a competent functionary and society into an administrative society. It seeks to *Mandarinize* society.

The defenders of miniaturization, of "alternative technique," believe that they are fighting the alienating megalomania of apparatus, and that they are returning to human dimensions. If the small action group, the small business, the individual wind-turbine, the ecological vegetable plot, the cooperative family, seem for them a return to more adequate human proportions, then they are mistaken. The tiny is even less human than the gigantic. The gigantic may be at least "admired," but the tiny disappears from view, it is "worthless." The "small man" and "self-management" are even less human than the "big men" and the multinationals. Never before has man *ceased to be the "measure of all things"* so radically as with miniaturization. In miniaturization, man becomes a particle, "information data," "bit," or worthless entity.

It is possible to measure how worthless the "*uomo qualunque*" is, if we look at the mini-programs. They are valid for anyone ("*jedermann*"), not for man. Models, as ideals, were supra-human. The ideal shoe was imperative: the shoemakers must make such shoes, and men must

80

wear them. The model was the "norm" and normalized men. Those who did not submit themselves to the norm were "heroes" but lacked "virtue." In this situation man was not worthless: models kept him in sight, imperatively.

Models, as forms, were human products that sought to violate other men. The industrial shoe was projected for the foot that was convenient for production, and all feet, with calluses or flat, had to adapt to the shoe. That is why the shoe was uncomfortable: culture was experienced as a violation, as neurosis. But progress improved the shoe. The industrial gigantism was not superhuman. What was sought was not "unbound happiness" but moderate happiness, the "happiness of billions." In such a situation man was also not worthless: he was raw material to be modeled.

Mini-models, as information, are of extreme elasticity. The intelligent instrument adapts the shoe that it produces to any foot, no matter which, since the point-like structure of its program can wrap the foot like a net. Every shoe is a glove. But this does not imply that the human foot is the measure of the model. On the contrary: the shoe adapts to any foot, be it human, animal, or that of an apparatus. Everything falls into the models' net and cannot escape it. Its tiny meshes, the "bits," catch everything. *Every model is "good"* because it does not seek to adapt to the phenomenon: it seeks to grasp it. Hence the elasticity of models makes it so that they are no longer experienced as violations of man. Shoes no longer disturb. Just like Gulliver, post-industrial humanity is caught by the Lilliputian net, however, given the elasticity of the net, humanity is not aware of that. It feels itself "freed" from the violations of industrial models. In such a situation man is effectively worthless: he does not even wish to free himself. He feels good as a slave.

Ideal models were *values*. When the Industrial Revolution transformed ideal models into forms, it provoked the "crisis of values." The counter-revolution of "chips" overcame the crisis of values. Once it transformed the models of forms into information, it turned them imperceptible. Values disappeared from humanity's field of vision. What remains are no longer imperative functions. The microprograms undo the myth of models as they annihilate values. Thus, the shrinkage of models is dehumanizing. *It devalues life.* Life within a miniaturized context is absurd.

OUR CLOTHES

The terms "model," "modern" and "mode" come from the same root, "med-," which means *to measure*. This original meaning has been forgotten. For example: we no longer remember that "modernity" as the progressive modeling of models means "unmeasured." The meaning of "to measure" and "to evaluate" are similar. Measuring-rulers evaluate. The evaluative connotation of the term enumerated above is also falling into oblivion. The proof of this is that when we hear the term "mode" we think above all of clothing.[6]

In the case of women's *fashion*, for example, it is not a case of values. In the case of models of cars, it is possible to sustain the thesis that the models from the 1980s were better than the ones from the 1970s. The models of Einstein's physics may be considered as "better" than

6 "Moda" in Portuguese is the term used to designate current fashions, as it also used to be in English when speaking of "modes." The current use of the term "fashion" still connotes a mode of behavior, but that has also been forgotten, which in my mind further reinforces Flusser's point. However, for the sake of the text, I will opt for the literal translation of the term only wherever it makes sense, so that Flusser's play with the word's variations and its root stays consistent. Whenever the use of the term "fashion" is more appropriate, it will appear in italics as a reminder. [TN]

Newton's. But no one will try to sustain that the current models of trousers, that do not even have a pocket, are "better" than the preceding ones. In the field of *fashion*, progress has become even more "exempt of values" than in the fields of cars, of science or of economy. It has evidently become *absurd*.

However, it is possible to object that the values of *fashion* are not epistemological, as in the case of scientific models, or ethical as in the case of cars. That it is a case of aesthetic values. That *fashion* trends are comparable to trends in art. But even if we assume such a (doubtful) position, through *fashion*, progress presents itself as absurd. Tendencies in *fashion* observe ephemeral impulses that are in a large sense alien to aesthetic considerations, and its models are aesthetically inferior. If then, as we hear the term "mode" we think above all of clothing, it is proof that *we have lost our faith in progress and in modernity*.

This explains why the field of clothing is the first in which *progress has stopped to function*. This is the first field in which we have stopped being modern. The field seems to offer an image of chaos. Everyone dresses as they please and do not feel obliged to follow models. So that at first sight the field of clothing seems to allow us to escape social programming, and to escape from those apparatus that project the "haute couture" models in Paris and Rome and that transmit such models through the channels of *fashion* magazines and *fashion* shops, in order to first program the so called "elite" and afterward, the ever wider layers of society. It seems that we are escaping such irradiating amphitheaters, that we are "freeing" ourselves. But that is a mistake.

84

People do not dress as they wish to, but as they believe they should. What one sees is not chaos, but a *complex system* of uniforms. Uniforms for liberated women (free breasts), for anti-racists (afro-look), for the new left (hairy chest), for the new right (leather jackets), for intellectuals (turtle neck), for female university students (bed-linen and boots), for theologians "after the death of God," for pacifists, for businessmen, for followers of Krishna and for conservative politicians. In sum, what one sees is a *system of uniforms for those that refuse to walk uniformed.*

This system is a complex code. It allows one to decipher the clothes carrier. Whoever knows the code, knows everything about the carrier; their economic, social and political position and their philosophical and religious opinion. Therefore, the method of *multiform uniformity* is more efficient from the point of view of censorship than the method of Maoist egalitarian uniformity (everything blue). Within a scene that is programmed in this way, it is easier for the apparatus to retrieve the feedback of its programming than in China.

In other times the situation was different. Whoever wished to decipher the clothes carrier saw oneself obliged to read through the clothes and not the clothes themselves. Long ago, people walked around in costume. The false elegance of the suburban beau, the touching awkwardness of the peasant in his Sunday best and the ridicule of the Japanese tradesman in Western clothing, were in other times clues that allowed for the *unmasking* of man. Today the clothes no longer betray the carrier they *proclaim* him. There are no more masks to be demystified. The clothes are labels today, and are no longer lies. Labels are mottos, and mottos do not lie. They are neither real, nor false: they are usage modes of a specific program.

Today clothes are behavioral models that invite the message receiver to behave accordingly. In times past, the clothes carriers were receivers of models that were irradiated by *fashion* apparatus, today they are transmitters of models. They are *message channels* and are unaware of the emitters of such messages: these are beyond their horizons. The communicational function of clothing has changed: it functions like a poster and like a tin of conserve. The clothes carrier is an apparatus channel.

In other times there were *authorities*, the couturiers, which imposed the clothes models. These pyramidal authorities no longer dominate the scene; crisis of authority. People refuse to follow the authorities. The scene is proof that *to refuse authority does not imply the emancipation of man.* Invisible programmers now occupy the place of authority. The pyramid of *fashion* has been substituted by the amphitheater of *fashion*. This totalitarianism of multiform uniformity allows the programmers to *choose* between the available uniforms. The crisis of authority has not led to the emancipation of society, but as it allows for an apparent freedom of choice, it has led to the cybernetic totalitarianism programmed by apparatus.

The clothes scene may serve as a model in order to grasp the scene in other fields. These scenes, such as those of philosophy, art, politics and religion, but also the scientific scene, which is supposedly "exempt of values," offer us an image of chaos that is comparable to the clothes scene. In all of these fields the crisis of authority is prevalent. And in all of them the resulting chaos reveals, under careful observation, a cybernetically programmed complex system. In all fields, this is a complex fabric of orthodoxies, dogmatisms, engagements, and tendencies that are opposed to each other so that every field seems like a battlefield. An even more careful observation reveals this battle to be a mere illusion, since even the battle itself and its result are programmed to serve as feedback for apparatus. Every heresy, including the anti-apparatus one, is automatically retrieved in order to serve the functioning of the program. And everywhere, the retrieval method is free choice: the program makes available to every heretic an appropriate uniform. There is everywhere a *multiform automatic totalitarianism.*

The method of free choice, of *democratic elections*, applied by such totalitarianism, may be observed at its most advanced functioning in Washington Square, New York, that beloved stage of our culture: mature ladies are seen roller-skating and wearing tops with pornographic phrases. They cross by enormous black men wearing Nazi uniforms playing the accordion and walking with lap dogs that are covered with fake jewelry, and by young barefoot girls dressed in bed linen fabrics with purple and pink hair that are pulled by police dogs in glass collars. These characters have freely chosen their costumes. The spread of available options is widely open. What may be observed in Washington Square is free choice in action: programmed multiform totalitarianism. Because what is observed are not "originals" but *stereotypes* of absent and inaccessible prototypes. What is observed, is a *collage*, or programmed chaos.

The scene at Washington Square invites a comparison with the colorful scene of the main church square of the Gothic city. The grayish monotony that is characteristic of the industrial city has been superseded and the scene is once again colorful as it was in the medieval city. We have "style" once again. But the comparison is misleading. In the medieval city, the coloring was a manifestation of the multiplicity of aspects of common faith, of consensus. That was the multi-coloration of "Catholicism." At Washington Square it is more a case of permutations, a mosaic of several programmed prototypes. Instead of consensus, there is a program, and instead of faith there is functionalism. Instead of the authoritarian pyramid of the Church, there is the massifying amphitheater. The Gothic square was a multicolored *community;* Washington Square is a colored *mass.*

In fact: the gray mass of the industrial society has been overcome, but not by a multiform society. The gray rock of the industrial proletariat has been pulverized into multicolored sand. Its colored grains form dunes, obeying the winds that blow into the scene from outside. Free choice, in such a situation, is not a decision, but an *oscillation* of the many tendencies of the wind. The elections are not existentially, but cybernetically explicable. It is only in this way that the changing form of the dune may be explained.

The dunes, public opinion, are multicolored because the individual grain of sand is blown by the several tendencies, however programmed, in one direction and then another. The multicoloration of the scene is due to externally programmed impulses that oppose themselves to each other. The ever growing and astronomic quantity of the grains of sand allows for statistical calculations of their future movements. Every causal or finalistic explanation of the formation of the dunes is naive. Even though they are multicolored, the dunes of public opinion are "black boxes."

The question that they formulate is formal: where does its *input* come from? Where do the winds that accumulate the dune come from? Which is the program? It is seductive to want to anthropomorphize the question, to turn it finalistic. Who is the instigator of the wind? Who profits from them? Who are the programmers of all of this exotic clothing, the ones that substituted the modelers of *haute couture*? Who is it that programs hippie trousers and bikers' helmets? Where are the prototypes of all of these stereotypes "hidden?" Whose interests do these models serve? It is seductive to want to *politicize* the questions formulated by the dunes.

However, the answer given by the phenomenon will disappoint the "critics of culture." It will be a de-politicizing answer. The prototypes of our clothes are not hidden anywhere. In this case there is nothing to be "demystified." Although several people profit from using clothes, it is not they who program the scene. On the contrary: they are programmed to profit. Behind the program there hides no human interest at all. All of these prototypes emerged due to the stupid and absurd game of chance that becomes necessity. An apparatus that is automatic and autonomous from human decisions programs the clothes scene. The scene is constantly changing because the apparatus obeys the *internal inertia* that makes it constantly permute the elements, the "bits," that are in its program. The combination "Nazi uniform–accordion" emerged by chance, but emerged necessarily in the course of the game. There is no mystery, no purpose, and no cause, behind the scene. *The political question is answered cybernetically.*

Political critique reveals itself inoperable. What the *fashion* scene imposes is the attempt to decipher the code that manifests itself in it. Whoever is interested in modifying the clothes scene, cannot wish to act politically. What imposes itself in such a case is the application of a particularly cybernetic strategy, which is more adequate to the absurd rules of the game.

OUR IMAGES

Our world has become *colorful*. The majority of surfaces that surround us are colorful. Walls covered with posters, buildings, shop windows, vegetable tins, underpants, umbrellas, magazines, photographs, films, and TV programs are all in resplendent *technicolor*. Such a modification of the world, if compared to the grayness of the past, cannot be explained merely aesthetically. The surfaces that surround us shine with color because above all they *irradiate messages*. The majority of the messages that inform us about the world and our situation within it is currently irradiated by the surfaces that surround us.

It is the surfaces and no longer the textual lines that primarily codify our world. In the recent past the codified world was dominated by the linear codes of text, and currently it is dominated by the *bi-dimensional* code of surfaces. Planes such as photographs, TV and cinema screens and shop windows have become the carriers of the information that program us. The dominant *media* are now the images and no longer the texts. A powerful *counter-revolution of images against text* is underway. However, it is necessary to discern that in this counter-revolution, it is a case of an entirely different type of image that never existed before. The images that program us are *post-alphabetic* and not pre-alphabetic, as are the images of the past.

Linear *writing* (for example the Latin alphabet or the Arabic ciphers) emerged as a *revolution* against images. It is possible to observe this revolution in specific Mesopotamian ceramic tiles. They show the image of a scene, for example of a victorious king. The image is composed of "pictograms" that signify the king and his enemies kneeling. Next to the image the same pictograms have been imprinted onto the clay once more, but this time they form lines. These lines are texts that signify the image next to it. The pictograms in the text no longer mean "king," but mean "king in the image." The text dissolves the bi-dimensionality of the image into a uni-dimensionality and thus modifies the meaning of the message. It starts to *explain* the image.

The text describes the image as it aligns the symbols contained in the image. It orders the symbols as if they were pebbles ("calculi"), and orders them in series just like a necklace ("abacus"). Texts are calculations, enumerations of the image's message. They are *accounts and tales.*[7]

Images must be explained or told, because as with every mediation between man and the world, they are subjected to an internal dialectic. They represent the world to man but simultaneously interpose themselves between man

---

7 In Portuguese Flusser creates a play with the words "contas" and "contos." *Contas* can be translated as both beads and accounts and *contos* as tales or loose-change, small coins. Both allude to small things that can be lined up and strung together but that also point to a climate of linear narrative. [TN]

and the world ("*vorstellen*"). As far as they represent the world, they are like maps; instruments for orientation in the world. As far as they interpose themselves between man and the world, they are like screens, like coverings of the world. Writing was invented when the concealing and alienating function of images threatened to overshadow the orienting function. Or when images threatened to transform men into its instruments instead of serving as instruments for men.

The first scribes were *iconoclasts*. They sought to break and pierce the images that had become opaque, in order to turn them once again transparent for the world. So that the images could once again serve as maps, instead of being "worshipped." The scribes' revolutionary engagement is clearly seen in Plato and the prophets: they *demythologized* images.

The gesture to read and write texts happens at a level of consciousness that is *one step* removed from the level in which images are ciphered and deciphered. For image-consciousness the world is a *context of scenes*: it is experienced and known via bi-dimensional mediations or surfaces. For textual-consciousness the world is a *context of processes*: it is experienced and known via the mediation of lines. For the consciousness structured by images, reality is a *situation*: it imposes the relation between its elements. This consciousness is magical. For the consciousness structured by texts, reality is a *becoming*: it imposes the question of the event. This consciousness is *historical*. With the invention of writing, history begins.

However, writing did not eliminate images. The history of the West (of the only "historical culture" *sensu stricto*), may be seen as a dialectic between image and text. "Imagination" as the ability to decipher images and "conceptualization" as the ability to decipher texts, are mutually superseded. Conception becomes progressively more imaginative and imagination more conceptual. Western society can be divided into two levels: the basic level, that of the illiterate that live magically (the serfs) and the level of the literate that live historically (the priesthood), or the level of images and the level of texts. And there is feedback between the two levels: images illustrate texts and texts describe images.

The invention of the *printing press* and the increase of general literacy through *compulsory schooling* dramatically modified this dialectic. Texts became cheap and accessible, first to the bourgeoisie and then the proletariat. Historical consciousness became accessible to Western society as a whole and was superimposed onto magical consciousness. Images were expelled from everyday life into the "*baux-art*" ghetto. Historical images, and above all the scientific ones, became unimaginable. Texts became "purely conceptual." Thus texts betrayed the intention that created them: they no longer explained or demythologized images. They were no longer de-alienating and started to follow their own internal dynamic, which is the linearity of the discourse.

Texts, as all other mediation, including images, obey an internal dialectic. They represent the world and conceal the world, they are instruments to orient but form opaque walls in libraries. They de-alienate and alienate man. Man may forget the orienting function of texts, which is their intended aim, and may start to act in function of them. This inversion of the relation "text-man," such "textolatry," characterizes our history in its last stages. Political ideologies are examples of this type of madness. Thus historical consciousness gradually lost the ground that supports it, the contact that the texts establish with the world of concrete experiences. And this contact happens only when texts explain images, when they have imaginable messages. The 19th century is therefore the stage for the *crisis of historicity*.

That was when photographs were invented, with their several variations; films, videos, holograms, etc. In sum: *technical images*. They are instruments for turning the messages of texts imaginable. Texts were originally aimed against images, in order to turn them transparent for our concrete lived experience, with the aim of freeing humanity from hallucinatory madness. Technical images have a similar aim: they drive against texts with the aim to turn them transparent for our concrete lived experience, in order to free humanity from conceptual madness. The gesture to codify and decipher technical images takes place at a level that is *one step* away from the level of writing and *two steps* away from the level of traditional images. This is the level of *post-historical* consciousness. This is a level that is still difficult to sustain. It is far too new in order for us to occupy it, unless for fleeting moments. We tend to constantly fallback into the level of historicity. We are, in relation to technical images, the same as the illiterate are in relation to texts.

Technical images are essentially different from traditional images. Traditional images are produced by *men* and technical images by *apparatus*. The painter places *symbols* onto a surface in order to mean a particular scene.

Apparatus are black boxes that are programmed to devour *symptoms* of scenes and to spew out these symptoms in the form of images. Apparatus *transcode* symptoms into images. The apparatus' program derives from texts: for example from chemical and optical equations. So that apparatus transcode symptoms into images in function of texts. They are boxes that devour history and spew out post-history.

Technical images *pretend* that they are not symbolic like traditional images are. They pretend that they are symptomatic, "objective." The difference between a symbol and a symptom is that the symbol means something to whoever has knowledge of the consensus of such a meaning, while the symptom is causally linked to its meaning. The word "dog" symbolizes and the tracks on the ground symptomatize the animal. This pretension of technical images of being symptomatic or objective is fraudulent. In reality, apparatus *transcode symptoms into symbols*, and they do it in function of particular programs. The message of technical images must be deciphered, and such decoding is even more arduous than that of traditional images: the message is even more "masked."

The transcoding process done by apparatus may be observed with relative clarity in the case of *television*. This is a giant transcoding apparatus that irradiates images amphitheatrically. The individual TV apparatus are slots for their *output*, through which images are thrown into the private space. The apparatus as a whole also disposes of a slot for *input*, through which it devours symptoms and texts. The symptoms come in the form of tapes, covered with impressions caused by scenes, for example, videotapes. The texts come in two different forms. In the form of reports, scripts etc. that "describe" scenes, and in the form of programming, that in its turn is founded upon texts of scientific theories and ideologies. That is: the apparatus nourishes itself with symptoms and history on several levels. All of this serves as raw material for the apparatus. Inside the box that is the TV apparatus, this material is translated into images and irradiated. It is transcoded from symptom and history into post-history.

It is not that history has stopped "developing." On the contrary: *it turns faster* than before, because it is being sucked into the apparatus. Events precipitate themselves toward the apparatus with accelerated speed, because they are being sucked and partially provoked by the apparatus. All of history, politics, art, science and technique are thus motivated by the apparatus, in order to be transcoded into their opposite: into a televised program. The apparatus has become the aim of history. It has become a dam for linearly progressive time. *The fullness of times*. History transcoded into program becomes eternally repetitive.

Hence, technical images, as opposed to traditional images, do not mean scenes, but events. But they are, all the same, images. Whomever they program lives and experiences reality *magically*, as a context of situations ("*Sachverhalte*"). However, such magic is not a return to pre-historicity. It is not based on faith, but on programs. "Program" is "prescription:" writing is prior to it. It is post-historical magic, and history serves it as pretext. Whoever is programmed by technical images lives and knows reality as a programmed context.

97

Certainly: it is possible to transcend such a form of existence through the deciphering of technical images. But this demands a step back from technical images toward programing, not a step forward toward conceptualization that is characteristic of texts. It demands *a fourth step.* Historical critique, that which searches for the motives behind the technical images, will not emancipate man from them. So that the current counter-revolution of technical images can be overcome only due to a new faculty, to be developed, and that may be called "technical imagination:" the capacity to decipher technical images. This capacity is associated with formal thought; such as it is being established through informatics, cybernetics, and game theory. If we do not manage to take this step toward "nothingness" ("absent structure"), we will never emancipate ourselves from thoughts and actions that are programmed by technical images.

OUR GAME

We tend to perceive our environment as a context of games, as the 18th century tended to perceive it as a context of mechanisms and the 19th century as a context of organisms. For example: for the 18th century the human body was a machine, for the 19th century it was a vital collection and for us it is a game of complex systems. Or: for the 18th century language was a kind of clock, for the 19th a phenomenon that was alive and developing, and for us it is a game of words. This tendency of ours toward a *ludic* attitude has two sources. One of them is our praxis, which is that of a game of symbols. The other is the fact that we live programmed: programs are games.

As a consequence we take games for preferential models of knowledge and action, and we take the theory of games as "meta theory." This is observable everywhere and above all in the way in which we find ourselves in society. We no longer grasp our social existence as if we were the cogwheels of a machine, or as if we were organs, but as if we were pieces of a game. Social problems no longer present themselves in the form of: what are the forces that move society? Nor in the form of: what are the purposes that move society? But in the form of: what are the strategies that are at play?

Well, this attitude of ours is not only "mental," or interpretative – it manifests itself in our gestures. We act as played players. An especially illuminating example is provided by the gestures of the filmmaker, this type of technical image that programs, in part, our behavior. In order to grasp the "being-in-the-world" of the player, of the *Homo ludens*, it is worth observing the gestures of the *filmmaker*.

He has at his disposal a filmstrip, onto which photographs are ordered linearly, accompanied by a sound strip. This filmstrip is therefore a linear organization of audio and visual symptoms. This filmstrip serves him as raw material for the production of programs to be projected in cinemas. The producer also has instruments at his disposal: glue and splicer that cut and stick the filmstrip.

The filmstrip is, in its turn, a product of a particular apparatus. The filmmaker took part in the production of the filmstrip, before he could have it at his disposal as raw material. Other functionaries that took part in such a production were the "scriptwriter," the "cameramen," the "actors," the make-up artists and the light technicians. All of them functioned with interrelated complex functions within the film industry apparatus. Thus the filmmaker has two levels of functioning: in the production of the filmstrip and in the production of the program.

The first level functions correspond approximately to the level of historical consciousness and some of its functions are known. The role of the "actor" and of the make-up artist for example, is a historical role *par-excellence*. It is not so easy to find parallels for the roles of scriptwriter and cameramen in past history. The scriptwriter is a literate that provides pretexts for the fabrication of images. He is a character that produces history in function of programs. The cameraman is an even stranger character for the historical consciousness. He has at his disposal an apparatus that captures symptoms to be transcoded into images. In order to do it, he assumes several points of view in relation to the scene. All of the points of view are equivalent and interchangeable. His gesture is the manifestation of an *overcoming of ideology* – and ideology means the insistence on one point of view. In this the cameraman is similar to the photographer. But the photographer jumps from point of view to point of view, and each time he jumps he presses a button: his gesture is quantic and marked by successive decisions. The cameraman, on the contrary, slides from point of view to point of view. He has at his disposal an apparatus that allows "scanning," "travelling," and "close-up." He doubts, just as much as the photographer does: he does not insist on a point of view. But he doubts without ever having to decide. This is the methodical doubt that is without parallel in history – a new form of knowledge.

Thus the filmmaker participates in the function of all of these characters. He directs these functions, having in sight not the event but the filmstrip to be produced. He does not conceive of the event as being meaningful in itself, but as the meaning of the filmstrip. And the filmstrip is for him raw material for the production of a program composed of symbols. So that for him the event means symbols. This inversion of the vector of significance is characteristic of the programing activity.

Once the filmstrip thus produced is in the hands of the filmmaker, he sees himself confronting a linear code composed of clear, distinct, and therefore calculable elements. His aim is to transcode this code so that, thanks to illusion, it starts to move. Hence the filmmaker confronts potential history and does so from the *outside*. He transcends history in order to play with it. He occupies the place once occupied by God. Like God, he sees the beginning and the end of history (of the filmstrip) simultaneously. Like God, he may interfere with history from outside, to produce "miracles." But he is capable of acts for which the omnipotent God is incapable: he can repeat events, he can leap from the future to the past and from the past to the future, he can make it so that historical time runs in reverse, and he can accelerate events. Contrary to God, the filmmaker is a *composer of histories.*

Due to his praxis, the filmmaker *overcame the linearity of time.* The line of the filmstrip is for him a structure to be modulated. He can curve it into circles of eternal return, into ellipses, into spirals and into vectors. That is why it is a mistake to consider the action of the filmmaker as a kind of magic. The magician thinks and acts circularly, historical man linearly. The filmmaker thinks and acts in a way for which line and circle are nothing but two structures equally available. His consciousness equally overcomes magic and history.

The filmmaker's post-historical transcendence does not imply, however, that he has emancipated himself from the events. It is true that he plays with history and that he splices and glues it, but history, as raw material, offers resistance to his manipulating gesture. It imposes its own game rules. The important thing to grasp in this is not the classic resistance that every object offers, or its "perfidy." The important thing is not the resistance offered to the filmmaker by the actors, scriptwriters, and light technicians. The resistance that counts here is of a new type. As he manipulates the filmstrip, the filmmaker must take into consideration the structure of the apparatus in function of which he is operating. He must consider the technical, financial, ideological and "aesthetic" demands of the apparatus, in sum: its program. The filmmaker produces programs in function of meta-programs. In that he distinguishes himself from God. In that he is a programmed programmer, a played player. He transcends history, but transcends it in function of programmed events. He is a functionary, he is not emancipated.

Thus the gesture of the programmer of films is recognizable within the other fields of activity today. All the programmers, futurologists, apparatchiks, researchers of public opinion, marketing executives, ministers for planning etc., execute similar gestures. For all of them, events and history are nothing more than raw material to be manipulated with a splicer and glue. All of them aim to transform history into program. All of them are restricted to specific game rules, and they formulate their strategies in function of these. All of them function.

If we seek to distance this phenomenological observation one step further, and if we seek to observe the level in which such game rules are established, we

103

will come across more programmers that function exactly as the ones just described. The demand for an ultimate "programmer," for an "untouchable mover," is revealed as a futile demand. Such a demand reveals itself as a regression to the infinite. The games that compose the environment reveal themselves (all of them), to be object-games of meta-games, which in their turn are object-games of their own object-games. Thus our environment reveals itself as a context of games that are co-implied, and whose rules are co-implied. In such an environment we are all played players, *Homines ludentes,* and pieces of the game: an absurd situation.

The absurdity of the situation reveals itself if we concentrate our attention on the existential impact of the filmmaker's praxis. The filmstrip consists of photographs that are clear and distinct punctual elements, and that when projected onto screen, become processes. Well, our tradition provides us with two, and only two, fundamental models of reality: the "wave" model, for which reality is a process, and the "particle" model, for which reality is atomic. The first model may be called "Heraclitian" and the second "Democritian." Both models are interpenetrable. The wave can be considered as a group of drops and the particle a stationary wave.

However, the filmmaker's praxis has a different impact. It shows concretely the fraud contained within both models. Photography is a symbolic particle, fraudulent frozen movement. And the moving shadow on the screen is a symbolic wave, fraudulent movement. Therefore the question: "what is the fundamental structure of reality?"

reveals itself as naivety. The fundamental structure of reality is the one programmed by the program-maker.

This has existential consequences: the maker can freeze waves, that is, he can transform action into scene and actor into idol. He transforms the "hero" into a god. And he can equally make particles move, and transform scenes into events, idols into actors. He transforms God into a hero. This concrete experience of the ludic manipulability of the fundamental structures puts an end to every ontology. The question: "what is real, and what is fiction?" loses its meaning. *We have lost the sense of reality*, we live absurdly.

To live comes to mean to be part of absurd games. Every question in relation to the meaning of games becomes metaphysics in the pejorative sense. To want to know if this or that televised program is "live" or videotaped, or if the character on screen is a politician or an actor representing a politician, becomes an "empty" question. In face of every program, the question that emerges is not: "how real is it?" but "how does it function?" The question of reality and falsity becomes a question in relation to the produced effect. What interests us in programs is not the *input* but the *output*.

This is another form of insisting on the current inversion of the vectors of significance. The symbolic games of which we take part do not represent any universe of concrete experience, but on the contrary, this concrete experience represents games. We live our concrete experience in function of games. Games are our ontological ground and all future ontology is necessarily game theory. Everything is fiction, nothing is real. We are chess players who are aware that it is a game, but for whom to live means to play chess. Certainly: instead of elaborating new strategies or meta-chess games, we can overturn the board. But in such a situation we would not emancipate ourselves from the game: we would fall into the wholly insignificant, trans-ludic abyss that hides underneath the games. It is in order to avoid such a fall that we are *Homines ludentes.*

OUR DIVERSION

There are cultures that appeal to the *concentration* of thoughts in order to reach happiness. In Hinduism and Buddhism the method of concentrating our thought onto one single subject leads to meditation, which reveals the illusory nature of the phenomenal world and leads to a piercing of it toward reality. These cultures have elaborated refined techniques in order to make concentration efficient. Our own culture has driven toward opposite techniques: techniques that aim *to divert* our thought from particular subjects and thus to propitiate happiness. The entertainment industry has built a powerful apparatus, and the refinement of our methods leaves nothing to be desired in terms of complexity in relation to the techniques of Yoga.

However, it is possible to question whether concentration and diversion are in fact such opposite motions, as they seem to be. A historical comparison between the West and the East seems to undermine it. The techniques that the West elaborated during the course of its history, and which are the opposite of the techniques of Eastern concentration and meditation, do not seek to divert but to modify the world. So that West and East seem to illustrate the choice open to human existence. The East opted for the self-affirmation of man and ran the risk of losing the world. The West opted for the conquest of the world and ran the risk of losing itself in it. So that East and West illustrate, in a gigantic scale, the dialectic of human consciousness that Hegel called "unhappy consciousness."

Entertainment has no place in the dialectic between engagement with oneself and engagement with the world. It is a motion that runs perpendicular to the plane of the dialectic of consciousness: it diverts such a plane. It is neither an attempt to find oneself nor to find the world, but an attempt to break with the unhappy consciousness, with consciousness "*tout court*," by spilling oneself over the world as method. One abandons happiness as an aim, which one knows is unreachable, and one substitutes it with multiform distraction as an aim. Entertainment seeks to distract from the contraction about happiness. So that entertainment is the *relaxation of the dialectic tension* that characterizes human consciousness.

The analytic method of dialectics is therefore inapplicable to the phenomenon of entertainment. Such a method falsifies it. In entertainment, the dialectic opposition between "I" and "world" is diverted to an intermediary ground, the one of *immediate sensations*; which are neither "I" nor "world," yet. "I" and "world" are nothing but abstract extrapolations of the concrete sensation. When one experiences a sensation it makes one forget "I" and "world." The film, the TV, the sensational news and the football game divert consciousness from the dialectic tension "I/world," because they are anterior to both these poles. Sensation is more "primitive" than consciousness; it is anterior to the alienation between man and world. Because entertainment is sensationalistic, it reveals both "I" and "world" as specters that circle concrete experience.

In a situation dominated by entertainment as a vital climate, dialectic philosophy (be it Hegelian or Marxist) is no longer significant. It is not Hegel, but Husserl who provides the appropriate categories for the situation. It is not the "Phenomenology of Spirit" but Husserlian phenomenology that corresponds to our way of being in the world. Entertainment as a search for sensations is a tendency toward the widening of the "Lebenswelt," and that which we search for is quantity and not quality of life. We want maximum experience, to accumulate sensations, because in successive sensations we divert the consciousness of our alienation in relation to the world. We are in search of concrete experience, we are "returning to the thing," in order to suspend our consciousness of unhappiness.

It seems, at first sight, that to accumulate sensations is to store them. As if we wanted to keep the sensations in our memory. This interpretation of entertainment led to the concept of "consumer society," a society that consumes material and other sensations provided by the producing apparatus. As if society was the digestive apparatus of a producing apparatus. This would be a bad interpretation of entertainment. Mass society, that which entertains itself, is characterized precisely by its lack of memory, by its incapacity to digest what has been eaten. This lack of memory cannot be explained simply by the fact that human memories have become redundant, since there are other, better artificial memories. A more adequate explanation is that there is no memory, no interiority, where there is no "I." Mass society is not a digestive apparatus, but a *channel* through which sensations flow, in order to be eliminated without being digested. What characterizes mass culture is not consumption, but its opposite: the refuse or trash.

Entertainment is the accumulation of sensations to be eliminated undigested. Once "world" and "I" are put into parentheses, sensation passes without obstacles. There is neither something to be digested nor an interiority to digest it. There is neither intestine nor the necessity of an intestine. What are left are *mouths* to swallow the sensation and *anuses* to eliminate it. Mass society is a society of channels that are more primitive than worms: in worms there are digestive functions. The "worm-like" feeling, by which we are sometimes taken over, is an optimistic sensation. Concrete sensationalism is more primitive than worms.

In the entertainment society, only the oral and anal apparatus function, only the *input* and the *output*. This is a counter-revolution of the *anal and oral libido* against the genital one. In entertainment, pleasure is focused at the mouth and anus. Life is directed toward oral sensation (to swallow) and anal sensation (to defecate). The genital categories (love of others and reproduction) are "overcome."

This allows for the apparatus that program us to use us as feedback. They can feed us with sensations that have already been eliminated, since we do not notice that we

110

have eaten them in the past. Every sensation is concrete, therefore always new. *We are channels for eternal repetition.*

Nevertheless: despite the counter-revolution of the oral-anal libido, despite our programming to be channels of feedback, there still persist in us some remains of interiority. These manifest themselves in two forms. One is the interest that the refuse awake in us: the awareness that we are being fed *shit*. The other is our tendency to stir the shit. The first coprophilia becomes visible as "*nostalgie de la boue,*" as the wave of kitsch and pornographies. The second one is more interesting.

There is the emergence of *coprophiliac sciences,* the study of the undigested. Psychoanalysis, archeology and etymology; the search for the "sources" and for the roots, are an example of this. There is the emergence of *coprophiliac movements* that aim to recycle the shit. The ecological movement is an example of this. The other is the recycling of specialists. The important element in this is the restructuring of our thought and of our activity. Since we are channels with mouth and anus, we think and act cyclically. No longer: "past-present-future," but "past-present-future-past." No longer: "nature transformed into culture" but "nature transformed into shit, transformed into nature." Such cyclical thought and action are symptoms of a semi-conscious interiority in relation to our re-programming into feedback channels.

The apparatus have not been able to divert us completely from this conscience, because before the re-programming, we were exceptionally conscious of ourselves and the world. Science accumulated a colossal amount of information about the world, and the acts of

111

the recent past have awakened within us a colossal bad conscience in relation to ourselves. It is very difficult to divert a well-informed criminal. That is why the apparatus are obliged to employ *extreme entertainment methods*. They hammer our unhappy consciousness day and night with a bombardment of sensations. And they manage to divert us with all of this only because we collaborate with them. We want to be entertained and we demand ever more intense entertainment, because we cannot stand to be confronted with our unhappy consciousness.

Consensus, thanks to which we allow the apparatus to entertain and program us into sensation channels, is founded on bad conscience and not on faith. Sensationalists of good faith are hedonists. They believe that the highest Good lies in the immediate experience. Such a consensus of good faith existed in the past, for example in Epicurean Hellenism. This is not our case. We are not hedonists, we are not Epicurean, not even Stoics, which is the other side of the same coin. We are convinced that the highest Good does not lie in the sensation. Our consensus preaches that sensation is surrogate to all that is good, of which we are convinced is unreachable. Our consensus preaches that sensation serves as a diversion from an unreachable good.

We continue to be convinced that there are rights such as freedom, justice, and human dignity. But we have learned the hard way that every attempt to realize such rights leads to the opposite of what was intended. That it leads to slavery, injustice, and indignity. This is the lesson that we are obliged to learn from the *socialist revolutions* of the recent past. The disillusion of these revolutions, that were the West's last attempt to escape

112

the resulting totalitarianism of apparatus from the Industrial Revolution, which also sought the same rights, is an experience that sticks deeply within our unhappy consciousness, from which we seek to divert ourselves. We are counter revolutionaries, we seek diversions because we are conscious that every future revolution will have the same effect as past ones: slavery, injustice, and indignity. Our consensus, be it explicit or implicit, that entertainment is the best method in order for us to avoid unhappiness, preaches thus: the apparatus society that entertains us is evil, but it is better than late capitalism's societies and the "popular democracies," if taken seriously.

Our entertainment is a game. A kind of *jigsaw puzzle*. The individual sensations that we devour form mosaics that vaguely structure themselves as images. Our consciousness is pulverized in the course of the game, and recomposed according to taste by chance. The entertainment industry programs chance. We experience every sensation casually. Every sensation that happens by chance is welcome. It serves to entertain us.

As a result, this has a curious consequence. Nothing is taken seriously, *everything entertains us*. Not only the programs aimed explicitly at entertainment. We devour everything with sensationalist attitude. Art, philosophy, science, politics, including the events that relate to our concrete experience: hunger, sickness, and oppression. Our work entertains us. Our human relations entertain us. We are incapable of seriousness, because what we want is the concrete sensation in exchange for the symbolic games of which we take part. Since these games no longer mean the concrete sensation, then it no longer has meaning. We live absurdly.

Apparatus have codified the world in order to entertain us. They have turned the world "spectacular." They are now seeking to sensationalize our own death. They have already sensationalized the deaths of others. They have overcome mourning. They have turned the death of others into kitsch. They will turn our own death into kitsch. Once this has been reached, we will have been reprogrammed. Our unhappy consciousness will finally rest. Programmed life shall be totally entertaining. This is the aim of the programs with which we are collaborating.

OUR WAIT

Pre-industrial society waited for the harvests, the industrial society waited for progress. Today it's not the wait, but dread that characterizes us. The three societies have three distinct existential climates in relation to the experience of time: the climate of agriculture is that of *patience*, the climate of industry is that of *hope*, and ours is that of *boredom*. In agriculture there are two periods: the one of estival action and the one of wintry passivity, which is the wait. In industry, there is the progressive transformation of the environment, and it is expected that such transformation is an improvement. Today we expect apparatus to function according to a program. This type of expectancy is relatively new and deserves to be observed phenomenologically with the aim of grasping our experience of time.

In order to be able to live in the post-industrial society, it is necessary to have "documents." These are symbols that allow the apparatus to verify in which of the departments the bearer functions. Every "citizen" has the *right* to such documents, and the apparatus has the *obligation* to provide them. However, "right and

115

obligation" are political categories, turned anachronistic by the functionalizing of society. They no longer function. So that whoever has the need for such documents has to execute particular gestures that are appropriate to the functioning of the apparatus.

The specific apparatus has to be fed particular papers covered with symbols, archaically called a "request," in the hope that it will spew out the sought document. The apparatus is programmed to do so. These requests must be filled in according to the rules of the game of the apparatus. The rules are formal, and have nothing to do with the document in question. The request papers must be of a specific format, the letters that cover it must be of a specific type, the papers must contain specific printed questions, which must be answered in a specific style. These papers, called "forms," must be obtained at specific slots of the apparatus, and in order to obtain them, it is necessary to request them. In this, the spiral circularity of functionalism reveals its absurd regression to infinity. In practice, however, the apparatus spews out the forms with relative smoothness. Once the forms are filled in and fed into the specific slot for *input*, the requesting party waits for the programmed functionality: for the ejection of the required document via the slot for *output*.

The requesting gesture has a "staccato" structure: every motion is followed by "pause" and wait. This is the characteristic gesture of automation and it has a quantic, "bit-like" character that constitutes a *mosaic of acts*. It is made up of "actomes." For example: some requests must have photographs. Specialized apparatus called "photo-automats" spew the photographs out. These provide programmed photographs: programmed format, color, background and lighting. The functioning of the photo-automat works in the following manner:

They are black boxes with slots. In one of the slots a coin is placed. This turns the light on and allows for the requesting party to enter through another slot. Now one finds oneself within a chamber that is reminiscent of a prison, and that has a chair that is reminiscent of that of a torture chamber. The requesting party sits on the chair with a programmed attitude and presses the button that is at arms reach. Following that, one smiles idiotically in the direction of the wall, and waits until the light that is inside flashes ironically three times. Afterward, one exits the box and waits outside for two minutes. On the outside of the box there is a user's manual that tells how long the waiting time is. If the box functions as programmed, once the two minutes have passed, through another slot, three photographs still covered in apparatus juice come out and the requesting party collects them. And following that, one fixes them to the request forms.

It would be absurd to want to contemplate the photographs. They are technical images whose messages are aimed at the apparatus and not at the one portrayed, or at any other "natural" person. Equally absurd would be to shake the box if it does not function according to the program. Every revolutionary act would be absurd. What is needed in such a case is to request from another department in the apparatus that a specialized functionary fixes the photo-automat to make it function.

What is important in this observation is the verification that the slots in the apparatus correspond to slots in the gesture: *slots of time*. The gesture has the "bit-like" structure of the apparatus program: it has intervals. These intervals are waiting time. Thus, for historical, processual consciousness, these intervals are difficult to bear. They seem empty. They do not allow a place for either patience or hope. Hence in extreme cases when the life of the requesting party may depend on the functioning of the photo-automat, for example when it is a case of obtaining a passport that allows the escape from the threat of a police apparatus, the two minute interval cannot be filled with hope. It is *tediously long*. This boredom is independent from the objective extension of the interval. Objectively, the photo-automat shortens the time between the taking of the photograph and its production more radically than the Concord has shortened the time between São Paulo and London. However, such objective progress is existentially uninteresting in both cases. What is important existentially in both cases is that the interval is an empty, still space, the *nunc stans* of antiquity that generates the *sensation of nothingness*. Boredom is the temporal experience characteristic of functionalism.

This is the current form of waiting. A tedious interval without patience or hope. The miniaturization of death. Thus it is obvious that this new temporal experience demands that we elaborate new models.

In the agrarian society time is a *cycle*: the eternal return seed-harvest-seed, day-night-day and birth-death-birth. Time circles in space and puts things in order. It replaces things into their right place, from which they have distanced themselves. To distance oneself is injustice, "*Adkia*;" man, in the course of life, dislocates things,

118

commits injustices. Circular time, destiny, replaces things into the pre-established order. It recriminates. It punishes. If man wants to escape the deserved punishment, then there has to be a sacrifice, a payment of fines. Man lives *magically*. Circular time does not allow space for causality. Day is the cause of night and the effect of night. It is the same thing to say that the sun awakens the cockerel, as it is to say that the cockerel awakens the sun: the circular model of time is *mythical*.

In the industrial society time is a *straight line*: a sequence of events that flows univocally, and that never repeats. No day is a repetition of the previous one, every harvest is singular and if there is life after death, it will be different from the one we know. Linear time is "historical:" it progresses toward the new. It comes from the past and demands the future. As it flows, it drags things with it. Every lost moment is definitely an opportunity lost forever. Every moment urges. Every act is irreparable. It will be the cause of unpredictable but necessary effects, that is: irrevocable. Nothing is, everything becomes. That is why there is no present. The present is nothing more than a point without dimension on the straight line of time. It has already passed as it happened. It is the time of *historical* life, and its model is the one of *causality*.

In the post-industrial society time is an *abyss*: a vortex in the present that sucks everything. The present is the totality of the real. In it all virtualities are realized. They "present" themselves. And the present is standing still. Wherever I am, there, the present is. Everything happens in the present, everything presents itself. Time no longer flows from the past toward the future, but flows from the

119

future toward the present. And the future is no longer at the end point of a straight line: it is the horizon of the present, and it surrounds it on every side. Wherever we look, there, the future is. There is no more progress, or Avant-garde. Every act is a gesture through which I reach for the future in order to present it. No matter in which direction I act. And there is no past as in the linear model: what happens is not the yesterday, but the tomorrow. The past is nothing but an aspect of the present. Things that have been presented are stored in the present. This present storage is the "past" in two ways: it is available (memory), or unavailable (repressed). The past is present in both these forms. So that it does not serve to "explain" the present, the present is what "explains" it.

Hence, the post-industrial model of time has the following dynamic: wherever I am, there, the present is. I am a vortex that sucks in the future in order to present it and transform it into the past. I am the abyss into which time precipitates itself. I am the vacuity. And I experience such vacuity that I am when nothingness presents itself during the intervals in my functionality. We may observe such a model, as we may visualize the preceding ones. The agrarian may be visualized as the orbit of the sun and the moon. Industrial time may be visualized as a river. Post-industrial time may be visualized as a magnetic field. And boredom may be visualized as a magnetic field from which the iron shavings were removed. Given our experience of time, this model imposes itself on all fields. It is the *cybernetic* model of time.

The foundation of this model is the experience of waiting within empty time. Which is the experience of our own vacuity. Heidegger and Sartre's existential analysis seek to grasp it. They seek to show that existence is a need that is surrounded by things that are full, extremely full of themselves, and which precipitate themselves into our need. However, these analyses do not grasp, as Camus' does, the *absurdity* of vacuity. They suggest that the waiting time is "availability" followed by "decision" and by "engagement." The experience with the photo-automat undermines such an analysis of waiting. As we wait thus, we are available for the apparatus. We cannot decide anything and every engagement in favor or against the apparatus would be absurd. Waiting is experienced as boredom, precisely for being an absurd interval in an absurd functionalism.

The wait, time standing still, reveals that we are slots. As we confront nothingness, we discover that we are nothing. That I as well as the world are nothing but abstract extrapolations of the concreteness of the experience of nothingness. During the wait, we make "*epoché*" in the Husserlian sense. Thus during such moments we grasp the function of apparatus. They function in order to fill the slots that we are. Since the experience of vacuity is the experience of death, we may reformulate the function of apparatus. They function in order to divert us from the experience of death. Within the slots of such functioning, death appears under the form of boredom. And the apparatus bombard boredom with sensations, with the aim of repressing it. Boredom is the enemy of functionalism, because it unmasks it. *Boredom is the demystification of the apparatus.*

There is a "bossa nova" that sings of a functionary that waits for the five o'clock train, while his wife waits for him at home with the dinner and in her womb a child waits to be born in order to wait for the five o'clock train. This is the phenomenological description of waiting in times of functionalism. That is what we wait for and what awaits us. That is what the futurologists calculate and what the planners program. However, these calculations and programs cannot obviously count with the *unexpected*. Despite the theories of catastrophes, the unexpected is unpredictable. And everything that is unexpected is terrifying. Because only the unexpected is capable of transforming our current form of waiting. So that we hope that the unexpected, the catastrophe, happens. We hope for that which terrorizes us. During such expectancy *hope and dread amalgamate*. This is the fundamental "balance of terror" under which we live.

OUR DREAD

Our situation is on a level of *stupidity* as never seen before. Idiotic objects surround us: plastic pens, electric toothbrushes, illustrated magazines, poster adverts, etc. Public discussions in the so-called "free world" can only compete in stupidity and superficiality against the propaganda in the so-called "popular democracies." If the intellectual level of our codified world was to be submitted to an intelligence test, we would probably verify that its IQ lies somewhere in the scale between idiotism and cretinism. This fact is not surprising. Apparatus, which have been defined as "super-fast idiots," have codified our world–*thus nothing is more terrible than stupidity.* Nothing deserves to be dreaded more.

These idiotic objects, these "gadgets" that surround us, program us in two different ways. We are programmed so that we can no longer live without them and we are programmed in order not to notice their stupidity. We are programmed to not be able to live without cars, and the oil crisis illustrates how this dependence of ours influences multiple fields, apparently independent from transport. And we are programmed not to notice that the car is a stupid instrument of transport, easily exchangeable for a more suitable vehicle. The first programming has as effect the degradation of our intellectual level and with it our aesthetic and political levels too. The "gadgets" are not toys for normal children, but for retarded children. The second programming has as effect our incapacity to concentrate our attention upon the roots of the stupidity that surrounds us: to analyze, for example, the epistemological and ontological aspects of the energy crisis. Society is in a process of progressive cretinization, or *dementia præcox*.

This dementia is verifiable above all in the so-called "elites." Never before has so much intelligence, discipline, imagination and resources been mobilized for the invention of idiotic objects. Never before has the economy been planned and directed with more stupidity than it currently is. Never before have political and social decisions been in the hands of such stupid people as they currently are. Historical tradition teaches us that we must dread the bad intentions of the dominant elite, and tacitly assumes that the elite pursues its malicious intentions with intelligence. So that this tradition sees in the revolutionary act a struggle between Good and Evil, and both as being intelligent. However, this is currently an inapplicable model. The apparatus and their functionaries are not malicious: they are idiots. And those that contest them are no more intelligent. The struggle that imposes itself today is against stupidity, be it from the "right" or be it from the "left." This is the *mortal danger* that threatens us.

The celebrated ontological analysis to which Heidegger subjected instruments ("*Zeug*"), affirms that they are things

("*Dinge*") that have been produced in order to attest man ("*bezeugen*"). Therefore, instruments emancipate man from his condition ("*Bedingung*"). Man would produce "culture" (the collection of instruments), in order to emancipate himself from "nature" (the collection of things). Gadgets, or "instruments" in the Heideggerian sense, undoubtedly surround us. They attest to our existence. But instead of emancipating us, they program us. *Today, culture has started to attest to human stupidity.*

Culture conditioned man, always and everywhere. The transformation of nature into culture has been, always and everywhere, the substitution of one type of conditioning for another. Instead of dreading tigers, we dread the police, and instead of dreading droughts we dread the crash of the stock exchange. However, despite this, the engagement against nature in favor of culture has been, always and everywhere, a dignified engagement. This is because the cultural conditions were, always and everywhere, effectively emancipatory if compared with nature. We may decipher instruments as "other men's deeds;" we are not obliged to assume them as "given." Thus our dread of the police and of the stock exchange crash could become a revolutionary act that transforms deeds. The engagement against nature in favor of culture has been, always and everywhere, an engagement in favor of the transformation of objects into instruments and of instruments into channels of human emancipation. This is the meaning of *engagement with freedom.*

This is no longer the case. Gadgets are instruments that are falsified when deciphered as "human deeds." They are *deeds of apparatus.* They are the result of the automatic manipulation of things even though specialized human functionaries participated in the manipulation. The deciphered man behind the gadget is not its producer ("*Erzeuger*"), but a function of the apparatus. What we decipher, behind the gadget, is the stupidity of the apparatus, which produces the gadgets by chance, if they are included in its program. There is no "intentionality" in gadgets; there is a game of chance and necessity. The danger of such stupidity is precisely that it results in *unintended situations,* and that it does so automatically. In face of such culture, every engagement in favor of freedom is no longer an engagement in culture. Not only in this culture but also in every culture, because every culture is a project that seeks this one.

This allows the formulation of our fundamental dread: we dread that *situations that were not intended by anyone will realize themselves* by chance, and that this situation of blind chance will become necessary in the course of the apparatus game. That for example, the atomic war will break out. And that it will break out as the result of an automatic process that is not influenced by human intentions at any of its phases. It would have been irrelevant if a prophetic political action had denied the financial means to the institutes that researched the atomic structure at the beginning of the 20th century: the scientific apparatus would have developed different energy sources that would be equally destructive. It is programmed to do so. It would have been equally irrelevant if an omniscient political action had stopped the scientific research of the 18th century. Our culture is programmed for the objective manipulation of the world, and it would have found

126

another method in order to realize such a program. The atomic war is contained in the program of the technical apparatus; whether it be military, economic or political, and these apparatus were contained in our culture's program ever since its initial project. The atomic war will happen by chance and it will not be intended by anyone, but it will *inevitably happen*.

The same is valid for all of the other dangers that threaten us. For the demographic explosion, pollution, depletion of natural resources, and the robotization of humanity. All of this is within the program. All of this is an aspect of the last phase of the game that is our culture. All of this is an "endgame situation," to speak in chess terms. What we dread, in sum, is the *endgame* of which we are players and pieces. Hence the apocalyptic, chiliastic climate in which we live, as well as our deep *counter-revolutionary* zeal. Because what we dread, is the inexorable progress of culture. Today, *to engage oneself with freedom*, and more radically, to engage oneself in the survival of the human species on the face on the Earth, *implies* strategies in order to *delay progress*. This reaction is today the only dignified one. We can no longer be revolutionaries, which means, to be opposed to the operative program through other programs. We can only be saboteurs, which means, to throw sand on the apparatus' wheels. With effect: every current emancipatory action is, when intelligent, a subversive action. Everything (terrorism, "alternative techniques," the green movement, women's lib, homosexual pride, alternative schools, alternative trends in art, anti-philosophy, and counterculture) is a reaction to progress. And everything that behaves progressively

127

acts in favor of the realization of the endgame. Every intelligent action today is a strategy of delay in face of the stupidity of progress. Not only of this progress, but also of every progress. Because every progress is the realization of a program, which seeks the end of the game. Delay and hesitancy are the only methods in order to postpone the end of the game: so neither Cesar nor Spartacus, but Fabius Cunctator.

The terror of our situation is the fact that the inevitable catastrophes that threaten us will be a product of chance. That they will be unnecessary, in the sense of being unintended: that the programmers of programs affirm, in good faith, that they seek to avoid them. This is terrible because it annuls the categories of historical thinking. For this type of thinking, "history" is the movement of the "spirit" in opposition to the world. It is therefore a series of deliberate acts. History is the spirit, the motion of freedom, turned into phenomenon. Thus history reveals itself today not as a motion of the spirit but as the automatic realization of programs. The "history of the world is the world's judge" in the sense of the execution of programs. And such programs are not "supra-human," as they are for mythical thinking: they are *infra-human*. And they are not "objective" as they are for mechanistic thinking: they are *stupid* because they are human projects that formulate themselves at levels that are inferior to the intellect. History reveals itself as human, not as a motion of the spirit, but of the pre-intellectual virtualities of man.

We cannot therefore engage with human intelligence against such pre-intellectual virtualities; we cannot engage in favor of "reason" because we know that reason

128

is within the program of such virtualities. We are counter-revolutionaries in both senses: we dread romantic anti-rationalism as much as enlightened rationalism. We know that they are both within the program and we know their realizations: fascism and the apparatus society. In other words: we know that intelligence has stupidity, which the stupidity of the heart ignores. This makes our counter-revolutionary zeal *ambivalent*. We are counter-everything. Our engagement with freedom is totally negative.

This is manifested through the *ambivalence of our dread*. We desire the catastrophes that we dread. And Freud made us conscious of this. Catastrophe theory affirms that a "catastrophe" is that point in the curve when the tendency changes structure and becomes unpredictable. Thus we wish that such a point be reached. "We expect the unexpected." Because we can predict, calculate and futurologize the curve without such a point, and hence predict the end of the game. This is absurd. There is nothing "beyond the catastrophe," precisely because "beyond" is unpredictable, unexpected, therefore not presentable. Our apocalyptic climate is not comparable to the climate of the year 1000. The end of the first millennium hoped for the Kingdom of God, and as for us, we do not hope for anything. It is no use to "objectify" our dread by saying that "there is always a future." Because "future" is an existential category: beyond the catastrophe we do not have a future.

The desire for a catastrophe (confessed or implicit) is *suicidal*. When all of the structures change, when all of the programs are re-programmed, we do not exist. Because we are *that* structure and *that* program. This becomes obvious in the Marxist motto: "to transform man." There is a presupposition that there is an unaltered structure: the dialectic one. No: at the sound of the trumpets, we will not all be changed, but annihilated. The desire for a catastrophe is not a desire for transformation (revolutionary desire), but a death wish (dark reaction): in itself a symptom of the endgame. The end of the second millennium is not like the end of the first.

Seen from "outside," our history presents itself as a kind of *Orestia*. We are "heroes" that precipitate themselves toward a suicide that was predestined by our crimes. But seen from "inside," it presents itself as the realization of an anti-heroic, cretinous program. Could there ever be anything more terrifying than a cretinous Oedipus?

OUR INEBRIATION

Never has there been a time or place when human life has been easy, this is because it has been, everywhere and always, life immersed in culture. Culture is simultaneously de-alienating and alienating, mediation and veiling, emancipating and conditioning. This ambivalence of the cultural environment in which man finds himself creates external tensions between man and his environment as well as internal tensions inside his conscience that are difficult to bear. That is why men have, always and everywhere, sought to *escape* this tension through inebriation. They invented *narcotic media*. These media are characteristic of human existence: man is not only a being that produces instruments, but also a being that produces instruments in order to escape from the tension produced by his instruments. The characteristic ambivalence of the relation "man-culture" also characterizes the narcotics that result from it. From the point of view of culture they are "poisons" and from the point of view of those who use them, they are "lifesavers." The term *drug* expresses this ambivalence: it means poison and medicine.

Drugs, as the result of the tension between man and his culture, *mirror* the specific culture that they provide an escape from. Opiates from the Far East mirror the religious experience of those cultures: they seek to provide a negative "enlightenment." Alcohol mirrors in some way our own culture, and hashish the Islamic cultures, and this could explain why Islam forbids alcohol but tolerates hashish, as the opposite of what happens to us. An extreme case may be exemplified by the Mexican culture. It is apparently a culture that has the narcotic as an aim, therefore an escape from itself as aim–a culture that seeks to deny itself through magic fungi. Within our current situation, in which the tension between our culture and ourselves becomes gradually unbearable, the allure exerted by Mexican culture could be explained due to this tension.

Given its ambivalence, the *ontological* position of drugs is slippery. Drugs are a medium for overcoming cultural mediation in order to reach immediate experience. Drugs are *the mediation of the immediate.* The inebriated man reaches, thanks to alcohol, hashish, and LSD, the concrete experience of the immediate, which is veiled for the sober man by the barrier of culture. He reaches, thanks to such media, the "*unio mystica,*" through which he dissolves into the concrete. He dives, thanks to such artifices, into the ineffable. Due to this ontological viscosity of the drug, the spectacle of the inebriated man is nauseating in the eyes of the sober man, and his ecstasy provokes repulsion in the sober man. Because the sober man recognizes in the inebriated man the contortions of meditation that seek to overcome all mediations and thus he recognizes in the inebriated man the contortions of all of human existence, including his own. The spectacle of the inebriated man is nauseating because we all recognize ourselves in him.

Certainly: any consideration of inebriation evokes the question of madness and art. The first shall be suppressed here and shall vibrate *sotto voce*. As for the second, it shall be considered a little later. What needs to be considered, above all else, is the *central position* that the problem of drugs occupies in the current scene. A position never before occupied. Apparently the use of drugs is a symptom of the profound modification through which we are going through.

It is a symptom in two senses: as a problem and as a discussion about the problem. As *discussion,* here is how drugs appear: everyone has formed an opinion about the issue, even though only a few dispose of sufficient information for such. The "well-wishers" condemn the use of drugs because it is detrimental to "health" (as in: assimilation into the established order). The "progressives" despise such a reactionary attitude and admit that drugs may provide new experiences and encourage fantasy. The "well-informed," the ones that read the para-scientific publications on the subject, discuss the difference between "hard" and "soft" drugs. The "political men" seek to profit from the discussion for their own aims. The "specialists" are condescending as they illuminate the ignorant mass. The institutes of public opinion publish statistics periodically about the consumption of drugs and about the oscillations of public opinion on the matter. The general *media* personalize the problem in a sensationalist manner. And, totally ignoring all of this, drugs are continuously produced, distributed and consumed according to the program implicit in our culture. This discussion therefore provides an example of today's overcoming of politics: the program makes the "awareness" of the problem redundant, as it does in other fields, namely the problem of atomic energy and ecology.

As a *problem in itself*, the question is this: to what degree is inebriation found within the program of today's apparatus? And how is it programmed? Which is the most functional method: to be programmed by apparatus in a sober state or an inebriated one? Apparatus already have at their disposal drugs that far surpass in efficiency the ones currently in use and discussed. With effect: although these super efficient drugs are known to many, they are not publicly discussed. They are, for example, chemical products that could be injected into the water distribution system and that would guarantee a specific behavior in society. Or technical methods that allow for the general *media* to subliminally program the receivers. Or pills that accentuate or attenuate tendencies in those who are super intelligent, criminals, rebels, or athletes. Unimaginable perspectives for the programming of society are as of now open.

The advantage of programming during a state of inebriation is a functionalism without friction. The advantage of programming via ideological manipulations or other, during a state of sobriety, is a less mechanical and more malleable functionalism. In the current phase, apparatus go through a learning stage thanks to which they learn *automatically* which of the two programming methods is preferable in specific cases. The learning happens through the feedback that our behavior provides for the apparatus. The problem of drugs becomes *automatically incorporated into the program.*

Apparatus function, in every case, with the aim to de-politicize society. They *objectively* de-politicize as they make society aware of the futility of every political action; and they *subjectively* de-politicize as they inebriate society's critical faculty. These de-politicizing functions act as tenacious pliers that crush the political dimension of human existence. The problem of drugs is on the subjective side of the way apparatus function. It is one more method in order to inebriate political consciousness.

Apparatus de-politicize as they occupy all of the public space. They privatize the republic as they deform all action into functionalism. Drugs, however, de-politicize in a different manner. People on drugs refuse to participate in the public space and they withdraw into the private space. To take drugs is a gesture that pushes away the republic, or that rejects it. It is not an a-political gesture, as functionalism is, it is an *antipolitical* gesture. The person on drugs not only does not participate in elections, but votes against them. The gesture of the person on drugs is not the gesture of a player that no longer plays: it is the gesture of a player that pierces through the game. That is why drugs are a problem for apparatus. People on drugs *emigrate* from the public square, not in order to function within apparatus, but in order to remove themselves. The problem for apparatus is how to retrieve them.

There are even graver problems. The gesture of the person on drugs, although a gesture that denies the republic, is publicly observable. It is a gesture of *protest.* In

135

this it is similar to a suicidal gesture: it publicly indicates the "beyond," not only the "beyond" of the republic, but also the "beyond" of apparatus. It is a public *scandal*: it demonstrates the possibility to transcend the apparatus. It urges therefore, from the point of view of apparatus, that the drugs be programmed and transformed into an apparatus function. As it is a case of being a technical problem, the apparatus are apt to resolve it.

The problem becomes even more complex, however, when in relation to a specific drug called "art." There is no doubt that art is a drug. That it is a medium in order to propitiate immediate experience. That it is an instrument in order to escape the unbearable ambivalence of cultural mediation and to emigrate toward a "better realm," as Schubert says in the Lied *An die Musik*, art sings. The ontological viscosity that characterizes every drug, characterizes art. This becomes evident if we consider the terms "artificial-artistic" and "artifice-work of art." However, in art there is an aspect that is missing in other drugs. Art, after having mediated between man and immediate experience, *inverts* this mediation and makes it so that the immediate becomes "articulated," that is: mediatized toward culture. Art turns utterable the ineffable and audible the inaudible. In it, the retreat of culture becomes an advance toward culture. The artist is the inebriate who emigrates from culture in order to re-invade it. To retrieve such gesture is not an easy task for the apparatus, because such a gesture is indispensable for the apparatus.

This is a movement that aims at the "beyond" of public space toward private space, and that grabs a piece of private space (an "immediate experience") in order to throw it over the public space in a codified form. This gesture may be *interpreted* in several ways. As a gesture that gathers "noise" and transforms it into "information" (this is the apparatus-like interpretation). Or as a gesture that transforms "experience" into "model." Or as a dreamer's gesture that transforms "ghost" into "symbol." But it does not matter how we may want to interpret the gesture, because it is always a gesture that, thanks to which, culture comes into contact with immediate experience. Art is culture's sensorial organ, through which it absorbs the concreteness of the immediate. The ambivalent viscosity of art is at the root of the ambivalent viscosity of culture as a whole.

However, this (rushed) ontological analysis of art certainly does not justify the deification of the "artist." It is not a case of creation "ex-nihilo." Art is not a gesture that dives into nothingness in order to return laden with something. It dives into the private and publishes it. And the private is also a "thing," that is: the public that has been repressed. Notwithstanding: art is a kind of magic. As it publishes the private, as it "turns conscious the unconscious," it becomes a mediation of the immediate, a feat of *magic*. Hence this ontological viscosity is not experienced by the observer of the gesture, as a repugnant spectacle – as is the case with other drugs – but as "beauty." And culture cannot forego this magic: because without this source of new information, however ontologically suspect, culture would fall into entropy.

Apparatus cannot, within the current situation, simply retrieve the gesture of art and transform it into

137

functionalism. If they were to inebriate such a gesture, they would become redundant due to a lack of new information. If they retrieved art, the apparatus would be condemning themselves: they would function at a standstill. And apparatus are learning this fact today, and they are doing so automatically. But in the cases where they are in fact retrieving the artistic gesture, they are *falling into entropy*. It is worth adding that the artistic gesture is not limited to the field that apparatus call "art." On the contrary, this magic gesture occurs in every field: in science, technique, economy and philosophy. In all of these fields there are those that are inebriated by "art," that is: those that publish private experiences and create new information. From the point of view of the apparatus, it would not be sufficient to simply retrieve this so called "art" if they want to reprogram the gesture. They would have to do it within every field of functionalism. Which would imply an emptying of every field of functionalism. On the other hand the apparatus cannot tolerate that the magic gesture should continue to be processed as it is. The gesture problematizes the apparatus.

The reason for this is that the gesture *re-politicizes*. Although its first stage is antipolitical, its second stage is eminently political. With effect: strictly speaking it is the only politically effective gesture. To publish the private is the only type of engagement in the republic that effectively implies the transformation of the republic because it is the only one that informs. However, in allowing such gesture, the apparatus endanger their de-politicizing function.

It is currently unforeseeable how the apparatus are going to resolve the problem. If they are going to opt for their own redundancy, or for the ever-present possibility of being themselves retrieved by man's openness toward the immediately concrete. And within this indecision of today's situation resides the fragile hope that we may, in an unforeseeable future, and through an unpredictable catastrophe, regain the reins of the apparatus.

OUR SCHOOL

The school is our heritage from pre-industrial society. Its name, "*skhole*," means "leisure." The opposite, "*askholia*," means "*negotium*" or business (the negation of "*otium*" or leisure). This contempt for an active life and preference for a contemplative life characterizes the school. It is the place for the contemplation of immutable ideas, a place for *theory*. And as such, the school is the aim of life. It occupies the tip of a vital hierarchy that consists of three levels. The base of the pyramid is formed by the *economic life* of women and slaves. Within it reins the eternal return of production-consumption-production, of work-tiredness-work. The intermediary level is formed by the *political life* of the free citizen. Within it reins the linearity of the bow ("*bios*")[8]: progress, from the idea to be realized to the reality to be idealized, up to the deed, which is the realization of the idea and the idealization of reality. The upper level is formed by the *contemplative life*, by the school. Within it, philosophy reigns.

Economic life is private, that is: "privy to ideas." It is an "idiotic" life, from "*idiotes*" = "private men." The political

---

8. Bow and arrow – the linearity of the arrow in flight. [TN]

life is public. The works produced are destined for the market in order to be exchanged publicly for other works. Contemplative life seeks knowledge through the vision of ideas. Economy justifies itself only for providing basis for politics, and politics justifies itself only for providing a basis for philosophy. Economic life allows the "owners" to dispose of free time in order to realize deeds. And these deeds allow an elite of philosophers to critique the ideas that were imperfectly realized in such deeds. In sum: *the purpose of politics is the school.* The philosophers that live at the level of the school are the kings of society. They are the "Scholastics" that guided society's behavior during the Middle Ages. The clergy are a victorious school.

The Industrial Revolution *deformed the school.* It distorted the original meaning of "theory." Theory became no longer the contemplation of immutable ideas and became the elaboration of ever more "adequate" ideas (models). School life was no longer contemplative. It stopped being the aim of politics because theory came to be a discipline at the service of active life. The hierarchy of forms of life was reformulated. The school became a place of *knowledge at the service of power*, a place to prepare for active life. Thus society no longer lived for knowledge (contemplation and prayer), but for the (industrial) realization of deeds. Hence, this *distorted school* became, during the Modern Age, a place for the elaboration of science and technique, and worked in favor of industry, that is, in favor of the owners of machines and political decisions. This explains the division of the school into three levels: the "primary" school, aimed at training the proletariat; the "secondary" school, aimed at training the

142

administrators; and the school for "higher education," aimed at the bourgeois elite, the one "responsible" for the progress of works.

Well, this modern industrial school is currently undergoing a *crisis*. It is becoming superfluous, inoperative and anti-functional. It is *superfluous* because apparatus program society's functionalism with methods that are superior to those at the school's disposal. It is *inoperative* because the modern school has an inappropriate structure for the current structure of knowledge and production. And it is *anti-functional* because the modern school functions badly within the reigning communicological system. This is the reason why we can observe everywhere, and above all in schools of "higher education," experiments that seek to "restructure the school." What is currently urgent is to re-think not only the meaning of "learning," but above all, the meaning of "theory."

The industrial school served two very distinct purposes. It served for the *transmission of information* to the future agents of the industrial process. And it served for the *elaboration of information* that allowed for the progressive improvement of products. Both purposes are currently superfluous. Information may be transmitted, with greater gain, to artificial memories than to human memories, because cybernetic memories store information faster and in larger quantities. It is unreasonable to wish to program human beings to compete with computers. And information can be elaborated with greater gain by cybernetic apparatus than by human minds. The apparatus that have been programmed in order to elaborate new models with the information that have been inputted, function more efficiently. And there is one other decisive advantage that the artificial memories have in comparison to human memory: artificial memories *forget* better than human memory. The temporal validity of models becomes ever shorter: better models substitute the previous ones with increasing speed. So that the models that have been learned must be forgotten in order to open space for better models. Therefore the need for the *recycling* of specialists, because cybernetic memories are recycled by the simple deletion of preceding information. In sum: the industrial school is *superfluous* because artificial memories learn better, think better and forget better than human memory. Men must be programmed with other aims.

The industrial school is structured according to the structure of the discourse of modern science and technique. It is made up of "branches" and every branch deals with a specific "matter." Thus the "branch" of physics in the school deals with inanimate objects and the branch of biology with animate objects. However, there are two exceptions in the school's structure: the "branch" of logic and the one of mathematics. These do not deal with materials but with methods, and they cross all the other school branches in a disturbing way. Because the structure of science, and that of technique, no longer follow the structural lines of the schools. New "formal" "non-material" disciplines such as informatics, cybernetics, decision theory, and game theory, are establishing themselves and are occupying the center of interest. Hence these disciplines no longer fit into the "curriculum" of the industrial school, since they "cross" its branches. The industrial school becomes *inoperative* because its structure no longer *mirrors the structure of post-industrial knowledge.*

The industrial school demands that the message receiver moves toward the message emitter. This is in direct contradiction to the current communicological structure. Today the messages are aimed toward the receiver and they invade his private space. Schools are theaters; current media are amphitheaters that irradiate their messages. The industrial school is an *archaic island* in the ocean of mass communication. It has become *anti-functional* because it functions in the opposite direction to the flux of messages.

So all of this allows us to visualize the *post-industrial school* of the future. It shall be an amphitheater that irradiates information toward future program analysts and programmers, which will function in function of apparatus. For example: it shall be a cable television system that will irradiate set theory instead of mathematical tables, or it will irradiate the syntactical rules of English instead of irradiating the lexicon of the English language. Future functionaries, thus informed, will be able to analyze or program computers and "word processors" instead of being able to calculate or speak English. Hence, the school of the future shall no longer program society for functions of mechanical thought, better executed by intelligent instruments, but for functions of analytic and programming thought.

This will imply a *new transformation in the social position* of the school. In the pre-industrial society the school occupied the tip of the hierarchy, in the industrial society the middle level, and in the post-industrial society it will occupy the lowest level. It is, in effect, the ultimate degradation of the school. It shall be the place for the programming of functionaries in function of the circular functionalism of apparatus. In Platonic terms: the school, originally a place for philosophy, became, in modern society, a place for active life and will become in the future the place for the economic slavery of the eternal return. According to the restructuring of the school, everyone shall become slaves and *totalitarian society* will have been established.

However, at this point in the argument, the problem of *new information* resurfaces, which was dealt with in the preceding essay as the drug called "art." The school of the future will necessarily allow openness toward immediate experience, even with the threat of totalitarian society falling into entropy. Then the dilemma that confronts apparatus programming reappears. This leaves two options: either the school of the future will function as described above, programming functionaries to program programs, in which case, even though these programs are "new information," they shall be nothing more than permutations of available information, and the apparatus shall function at a standstill. Or the school will allow the information receivers to withdraw from the school into their private spaces and from there publish effectively new information. In which case, the apparatus run the risk of being *appropriated* by the participants of the new school.

Creative inebriation, art, occurs within every discipline. Everything that man knows, makes and experiences, can become *beauty*, if it is informed by the plunge into the private. Every arrow is beautiful if it is a product of

146

"art," that is: a publication of a concrete experience, and it is because it is beautiful that it will be aerodynamically "correct," and "good" for hunting. It will be "a work of art." It is in this sense that man is a being "bathed in beauty" (Schiller), and that the "*kalokagathia*," the wisdom that the Good is beautiful, is the highest knowledge. Thus the school of the future will not be able to cover-up this openness toward beauty within any of the disciplines that it irradiates without running the risk of its own entropy, and it will not be able to allow for this openness without running the risk of its own overcoming by man.

The industrial school bypassed this dilemma, already sketched out, by instituting the "academies of fine arts." They are institutes that aim to create "artists," that is, cripples that have had the political and epistemological dimension that is proper to man, amputated. The opposite of these institutes are the scientific and technical schools of higher education that aim to amputate the aesthetic dimension of man and to create "pure" scientists and technicians. Thus the industrial school managed, although problematically, to repress the problem of creativity: it incarcerated "art," thus labeled, into a deified "ghetto" and managed thus to create an *ugly* human environment as the only cultural form of history. Suffice to mention the industrial cities of the 19th century.

However, this stratagem of the industrial school proved to be faulty. The apparatus revoked the isolation and sterilization of the aesthetic dimension. They retrieved "art" in the form of industrial "design," "media art," and political science, as if these were "art." The "pure artist" became an anachronism. The *original unity of truth, good*

147

and beauty became reestablished by the apparatus, but this time under the form of "know-how," of *technology*. With this strategy, the apparatus aim to recover the creative dimension of man, which threatens them. The school of the future should be an institute of technology; creativity at the service of apparatus.

These institutes, however, are ambiguous from the point of view of the apparatus. They shall necessarily irradiate *formal* disciplines, that is: to provide a vision of the subjacent structures. And this is "theory," closer to the meaning of it according to the Ancients. The Platonic academy demanded the knowledge of mathematics and music from the students, which are formal disciplines. The technological institutes of the future will demand the knowledge of informatics, cybernetics, set theory and game theory. This will provide the students an "ironic" withdrawal in relation to apparatus and their functionalism. And this theoretical distancing will be an invitation for a plunge toward immediate experience. An invitation to "philosophy." In other words: behind the backs of the apparatus, the students of the school of the future will transcend the apparatus. They will perceive the apparatus as a game. They will play with the rules that they learned. They will transcend function, not as a filmmaker transcends the filmstrip, but as the philosopher transcends the city. They will transcend the apparatus *theoretically and concretely*. Thus the technological institutes may become, dialectically, academies in the Platonic sense of the term. They may execute the viscous ontological *turning* that is *characteristic of art*.

148

This turning, if executed, shall be manifested by the fundamental restructuring of the school, which is not the intention of the apparatus. From discursive, it shall become dialogic: it will no longer speak "about" but "with." The "forms," the subjacent structures, shall no longer be "subjects" and will become *intersubjective strategies*. The participants of the school will then no longer be "programmed," and shall become dialogic apparatus programmers. *They will no longer program programs, but the apparatus themselves.* They shall live a trans-apparatus life. Totalitarian society will become a "democracy" in a way never before imagined.

A school where everyone is king instead of slave? Certainly: a remote chance. However, it is a possibility contained in the apparatus program. Will this possibility by chance realize itself before the apparatus have had the opportunity to robotize us in their new schools? Both virtualities are in the program. The program is contradictory at this decisive point. The strategy of hesitation reveals itself as not entirely negative: to delay progress toward robotization in order to allow for the *chance democratization of space and time.*

OUR RELATIONS

Today we tend to perceive the world that surrounds us as a context of *relations*, and not as one of *objects* or *processes* as used to be the case. The world is gradually changing from "situation" or "event" into "field." This transformation is not only that of models of knowledge. Our models of experience are equally changing: we are experiencing our environment as a net and this is becoming more obvious in relation to our experience of the society that surrounds us.

Society is being experienced and grasped ever more clearly as this *net of relations,* which not only makes us what we are, but *tout court.* No matter what I am, I am in relation to any other, and if I assume myself as "I," I do it because some random other calls me "you." I am "father" in relation to my son, "boss" in relation to my employee, "writer" in relation to my reader, and every other "definition" of my being-in-the-world constitutes similar relations that attach me to the social net. If, thanks to an effort of abstraction, I manage to "suspend" every definition, I will not have discovered any "absolute" nucleus that I could call "the essence of myself" ("soul," "identity"), but I will have discovered that the term "I" designates a type of imaginary hook, upon which hang the relations that I am. I will discover that once the relations that attach me to the social net are abstracted, I am strictly *nothing*. The relational view implies not only the discovery of the vacuity of objects and processes, but above all the discovery of the vacuity of existence in the world.

Thus it seems that this relational ontology results in an *altruistic* ethics and behavior. If all that I am are the relations that attach me to the Other, and if I am becoming conscious of this, it seems that I will behave in function of the Other. And if the pronouns "I," "you," "we," and "you" (*pl.*) are revealed not as persons' names but that of relations, it seems as though this consciousness will become "politicized" in the sense of an *intersubjectivity* that is responsible for the Other and by the Other. This seems to be the consequence of relational ontology, because "relation" implies the possibility of intersubjective dialogue, of question and answer exchange. Relational ontology appears as the "overcoming" of an individualistic egoism by a "super-individualistic" altruism.

In reality, this is certainly not what is happening. We are witnessing, on the contrary, a *massifying de-politicization*. The explanation for this surprising consequence of relational ontology lies in the *model* of field that supports our notion of "field." It is a dynamic, complex model. The family can serve as an example of how this model works: it is conceived as the composite of relations of the type "father/son," "husband/wife," "father-in-law/son-in-law." These relations are co-implied and ramify. The relation "father/son" implies the relation "grandfather/grandson," and the relation "brother/brother" ramifies into the relation "uncle/cousin." The family as a knot of relations is in turn related to other knots that form the dynamic and always changing fabric of society. Every relation has innumerable emotional, cultural, economic, political, biological, and ethical aspects that are inexhaustible. In sum: the family reveals itself as a *black box* never entirely explainable, and graspable only if we concentrate our attention on its *input* and *output*. It then reveals itself as cybernetically manipulable.

This is valid for all the other social categories, be it "class" or "people." They are thus revealed as knots of relations that form and deform during the course of the game of permutations, that appear by chance and that become necessary in order for the game to continue. Once the inherent virtualities of the *social game* have been exhausted, society decomposes, the knots become undone, and the final stage of the game emerges, entropy. That is: society becomes an amorphous mass. Thus the subjacent model to our notion of "field" does not imply altruistic behavior, but *ludic* behavior: not "political consciousness" but "social technique and political science."

Therefore not only do we conceive of society as a manipulable and transcendent game: we live it as such. We experience our social relations as causal encounters, as game moves. This is turning the social fabric extremely dynamic. We are moving within the social context with accelerated irresponsibility, and we run, during such motion, against a growing number of "Others." This geographic, economic, informational, intellectual, and sensational, social mobility of ours turns us ever richer, in

153

the sense that we involve ourselves in ever more numerous relations. Simultaneously, this mobility reveals, ever more clearly, the vacuity of the nucleus within which these relations concentrate. We are playing a growing number of roles in the social game, and we always know better that these roles are *masks that cover nothing.*

This irresponsible enrichment of social life represents "freedom" for us. We are free to tie and untie innumerable relations, and these relations become progressively lax because they always reveal increasingly better that they fundamentally tie nothing. Hence the growing enrichment of the relations that we are, this growing "freedom," is accompanied by a growing sense of loneliness. The social game is thus revealed as an *absurd game.*

The reason for this is that the "field" model demythologized society, it amputated society's mythical and historical dimensions, it *de-existentialized society.* This becomes obvious if we consider the concept of *fidelity.* This is a typical category of finalistic thought, for which society, far from being a relational game, presented itself magically and mythically, as a community of destiny. It was possible to distinguish in it two types of relation: the predetermined and the freely assumed ones. Man was thrown, by destiny, into predetermined relations (family, people, class), and created, by himself, free relations (loving, professional, friendly).

It is not that these freely assumed relations had ruptured the designs of destiny. On the contrary: they were the result of gestures that assume destiny. If a man and a woman met and fell in love with each other, this apparently casual encounter becomes revealed as

154

predestined. The relation that arose from the encounter, for example marriage, was a predestined relation. But was nevertheless a freely assumed relation. Because it was a relation based on fidelity. Fidelity is destiny's free choice, *amor fati*. Fidelity is the foundation of freedom, and *where there is no fidelity, there is no freedom.*

Hence currently the very concept of fidelity has become archaic and ridiculous. It occurs in kitsch films and demagogic discourses. Still, in the Middle Ages, fidelity constituted the very stuff of which society was made. It was fidelity that linked the knight to the ruler, the master to the art, the serf to the lord, and the disciple to the master. And above all it linked man and woman in marriage. Currently all of this is nothing but demagogy. We are not faithful, we are game partners: in the game of bridge, the sexual game and the functionalism game. It would be summarily ridiculous if we wished to maintain fidelity to the apparatus in which we function. Fidelity is a personal relation and apparatus are not people. Nothing is a person, with effect: not even the bridge partner or the partner in marriage. Everything is an apparatus, a black box. Our "field" model, the result of relational ontology, eliminates the concept of "person." We are incapable of experiencing, or even of conceiving, fidelity. Which implies that we are *incapable of freedom* in the existential meaning of the term.

This is the reason why the majority among us do not even resent the lack of freedom. The small minority that suffers the consciousness of the absurdity of the social game, has invented a substitute to fidelity, called "engagement," that can provide a sensation of freedom.

155

This minority recognizes that freedom is the gesture of assuming responsibility, and that this is the only strategy that endows meaning to the society game. Just like fidelity, engagement assumes responsibility. It sacrifices availability and social mobility in favor of a specific relationship. But there is a profound difference between fidelity and engagement. Engagement is founded on deliberate decision, and fidelity on spontaneity. No one decides to be faithful: fidelity is maintained. In archaic terms, convenient to the subject: *engagement is fidelity without love*. So that the substitution of fidelity for engagement is a symptom not only of our incapacity for existential freedom, but above all of our *incapacity for love*. And engagement is the gesture to assume an impersonal relation: we do not engage with an-other (man or God), but with "objects" (thoughts, acts, movements, ideologies).

Fidelity, as trust, is a *religious* category. The Latin word "*fides*" designates both terms. Fidelity is the active side and trust the passive side of faith. I am faithful to God, my wife and my friend because I trust them. Thus, given the crisis of trust, I am incapable of maintaining fidelity. But I may engage without trust. Because engagement is the deliberate act of sacrifice of critical distance. The current engagement of the conscious communists, for example the engagement of the defendants in the Moscow courts is a proof of this. To the contrary of what some think, engagement is not a religious category. It is a gesture of sacrifice that knows it is absurd and that aims to give meaning to what it knows is absurd. Engagement is a player's gesture, a deliberate strategy.

156

However, this analysis of our social existence does not reveal the whole truth. The new relational ontology, according to which we recognize ourselves as vacuities in which relations concentrate (be they centrifugal "intentionalities" or "intentionalities" that have come from the outside), imply a new opening in human existence. If we know that we are vacuities, and if we experience ourselves concretely so, is because we are open. Open toward death, toward nothingness, in a more radical sense than previous generations. The sensation of absurdity that invades us and which forms the base of our being-in-the-world, does not turn us only into players: it also turns us as thrown-toward-death. And the "field" model, the one of the black box, is not necessarily the only one that serves us in order to grasp our being-in-the-world. Another model is available.

Because of the opening that we know we are, and that we experience as an opening toward nothingness, we are capable of perceiving other openings in which we *recognize* our own opening. Vacuities that absorb our "intentionalities" and which project their own "intentionalities" into our opening. Thanks to this openness of ours, we are capable of recognizing in others, better than previous generations, our own absurd loneliness toward death. Certainly not of recognizing others as "people," but of recognizing our vacuity in others. If this casual and precious encounter is established, we are taken over by a "*sui generis*" inebriation: we recognize our own death in the Other. This inebriation is close to the one provided by the drug called "art". This is, with effect, an *ars amatoria*, which is subterraneously linked to the *ars moriendi*. It is precisely because we live

157

absurdly and are incapable of trust and fidelity that we are open to such inebriating, rare but "altering" encounters, in which the loneliness for death becomes a shared loneliness.

This suggests a model of the experience and knowledge of the Other founded on vacuity that has no parallel in the past. Endgame model. In this model, it is not a case of "wanting to alter the Other," but of being altered by the Other. This is not a "political" model in the historical meaning of the term. It is not a model to modify society. It is, on the contrary, a model that seeks to grasp the alteration that is processed within myself during such encounters. However, this is not the reason why this model may be considered as "privatizing," or "de-politicizing." On the contrary: this model allows to glimpse, even though vaguely, a new type of social relation, founded on the consciousness of the absurdity of human existence.

It is summarily uncomfortable to speak of such aspects. Uncomfortable because it is about concrete experiences which are, by definition, unutterable. However, is this not what characterizes the *ars amatoria*, as every art: the impossible effort to articulate the unutterable? Hence I believe that this art of love, in a situation that we know to be absurd, is the only answer of which we dispose in order to face the abyss that has opened under our feet, and that such an art cannot be deliberate, but emerges spontaneously. And I believe that it is the only alternative to suicide, since it is a suicide into the Other.

RETURN

The transition from the industrial society to the post-industrial is being processed in the so-called "developed" world. Simultaneously, the largest part of humanity is undergoing several progressive phases of industrialization. In the "First World," linear, historical thought, which is founded on texts, is being challenged by a thinking that is structured by post-textual codes, such as that of technical images. In the "Third World," efforts are being made to increase adult literacy. In Western societies, historical and political consciousness is giving way to a new type of consciousness that is still difficult to characterize. Non-Western societies are seeking, sometimes violently, to become political and to plunge into history. Current times are marked by the *discrepancy* between the established social forms, thought structures, and levels of consciousness.

This is not a case, however, of a simultaneous existence of different phases. For example, it would be a mistake to compare the current renaissance of Islam with that of the West in the 16th century, to compare Khomeini with Savonarola. This is because all of the currently

159

established phases are co-implied. Khomeini is Savonarola synchronized with cybernetically controlled oil ducts. This "overlap" of phases manifests itself tragically in the conscience of the Third World's elite. If these elites apply historical models in order to grasp the current situation, they discover the symptoms of the emptying of the centers of decision that manipulate the neo-colonized societies, and feel challenged to take over the reins of events. If on the contrary, they apply post-historical models, they discover the absurdity of such "political will," for which they know themselves to be programmed by the apparatus they aim at. The tragedy of the *synchronization of discrepancies* is that the First World has emptied the future of the Third World through the emptying of history by transforming it into a game. The Third World's elite may as of now observe, "concretely," what would result if they were to be "victorious:" not the emancipation of its society, but the totalitarianism of apparatus. And if they decided that the First World was something to be avoided, they would know that no alternative would be preferable to this one: they are, one and all, in the program.

This clockwork of disparate phases in current society and consciousness may be grasped if we make a distinction between two frequently mistaken concepts: the *new* and the *young*. The First World is characterized by the emergence of the new. The Third World is a young society if compared with the First World. In the First World there emerges the *new man* with a new thought, behavior and world-vision, never seen before. In the Third World it is the *young* that mark society. The First World is senile: it has *already* gone through the phases that the Third World

160

currently goes through. The Third World is archaic: it *still* has not reached the First World's phase and it is repeating phases already accomplished by the First World. The Third World is *Ancient*: in the sense of "Ancient Greeks." The First World is *decadent*: in the sense that Hellenism is the decadence of the Ancient Greeks. The Third World harbors virtualities not yet realized: it is poor in realizations but rich in virtualities. The First World has effected a great part of its virtualities: it is effectively rich and virtually poor. The tragedy of the young today is that they are virtually old. And the tragedy of the new today is that it is the realization of the old.

A superficial consideration of the current scene may lead to a belief that young societies are more *dynamic* than the old: that they are developing. This is a mistake. The new that is emerging in old societies is precisely the consciousness that the dynamism is nothing but one of the dimensions of the "real," that the process is nothing but one of the dimensions of the structure. The old societies are more dynamic than the young ones, precisely because they have overcome development. *History is nothing but one of the dimensions of post-history*, and the old societies live more historically than young societies. The difference between the two societies is not that the young ones have more movement. The difference is that young societies *want* to make history, while the old ones already have it, and no longer want to make it, but *do it* automatically. Young societies are below history and wish to *penetrate* it. Old societies are within history and history is within them, and they want to *leap beyond* it. For the young, the problem is the future to be conquered. For the old, the problem is the realized future, death. The young seeks to realize itself, the old confronts the aim of realization: the reality of death. The tragedy of the young today is that it has models at its disposal that formally point to the aim of every realization: to the exhaustion of every virtuality, to entropy, to death. And the new in all of this is precisely that the old exhausts the young within its project. In other words: the young is at the proximity of the *source* of linear time, and the new points to the *origin* of time, in which linearity is unmasked as just one of the dimensions of temporality. Currently, *the new is infecting the young.*

Therefore, the quarrel between the young world and the old world, which is currently centralizing all interests, is nothing but an external symptom of a deeper quarrel that lies within everyone's consciousness or subconsciousness. The border between young and new does not only divide society between "south" and "north." It divides, even more significantly, everyone's conscience today, be they African nomads or American and Russian functionaries. Today's *schizophrenia* is not only collective: it characterizes all of us individually. It is not that the more developed among us have "overcome" history: they harbor it even more significantly than the ones that want to become politicized. And it is not that the less developed among us are in need of post-historical consciousness, the awareness of objectifying manipulation: they are themselves victims of such manipulation, even more significantly so than the developed ones. The synchronizing clockwork of pre-history, history, and post-history that characterizes current times, grinds everyone's experience, thought, and behavior. Hence, that is why we are all so disorientated.

If we hold on to the distinction between "young" and "new" we may at least distinguish between two types of problems that challenge us. Between problems of the young, that are *ipso facto* old problems, for example those of "growth." We have models at our disposal in order to confront such problems. And problems due to the emergence of the new, for example those of programming. We do not have models at our disposal in order to confront such a problem. Therefore the new problems are what threaten the annihilation of all of humanity, that is: ultimate objectification. Not "the limits of growth," but "programmed growth," not the exhaustion, but the recycling of resources, and not the oppression of man by man, but the nuclear war. The threat is not the young, *the threat is the new*.

The new is horrifying, not for being so and not differently. The new is horrifying for being new. The new man that is emerging around us and within us, horrifies us, because we cannot sympathize with him in the exact meaning of the term. We do not oscillate with his vibration. His gestures are not ours. His models do not square with ours. We cannot decipher the codes through which he symbolizes the world. And, since we are, as of now, new men; we cannot sympathize with ourselves. We are out of tune. A civil war without precedent is being fought within us: the new that we are is rebelling against us. It is as if we were, each one of us, going through an agony that we experience sometimes as the final stage of a mortal illness and sometimes as a birth. The new is horrifying and we are ourselves, new. We are in the situation of Zeus when Athena cracked his head open.

The irruption of the new explodes the old. All of the millennial edifices that history built are crumbling. Family, class, people; science, art, philosophy; values, aims, beliefs; it does not matter in which field we wish to seek to lean on the old, everything is contaminated by the new. And in the place of all of these venerable structures, apparatus that are programmed by programmers are rising. Certainly: we are as of now, sufficiently new in order not to be able to cry for the disappearance of the venerably old: we no longer venerate it, we tend to have contempt for it. It has become transparent for our de-mythologizing gaze. But we cannot even welcome the new: we are still excessively old for such an undertaking. We resent the new, the negation of the soil in which we are rooted. The negation of the highest value of our historical culture: the dignity of the human subject.

In good conscience, we can neither join the new nor the old because both are repulsive to us. But what we can do is to abstain from this quarrel that simply takes place in our minds. We can take a step back from the arena, and *return* to the origin of the quarrel. In a nutshell, we can refuse every historical engagement and every functionalism in apparatus. Certainly: we will never be able to fully effect such a retreat. Ivory towers are expensive "*résidences secondaires*" and "dachas" to be built and maintained. And they will crumble in the earthquake that is being readied, just as all other edifices and shelters will crumble. However: several monasteries survived the irruption of the new at the end of Antiquity, and it was thanks to them that culture as a whole survived. Thus the aim of this retreat to the base is not the survival of he who retreats: it is the survival of man, according to the meaning that we are programmed to give to this term as disillusioned Westerners.

The decision to return is the decision to exchange the solitude of the mass for the solitude of the lighthouse guard. For solitude in the private space, where the concrete foundation reappears. Not therefore the private solitude of someone who cultivates their garden, but that private solitude in which God appeared to the prophets. The return here envisioned is the retreat to that private place from which it is possible to at least nourish the hope to be able to experience the concrete, and articulate it. Therefore a return to that base from which publication is possible. A return to a *publishable private*.

All of the preceding essays sought to grasp this turmoil of the private into the political, some explicitly, and the majority implicitly. They certainly did not manage to grasp it, given the slippery viscosity of such a leap from the concrete to the symbol that is necessarily abstract. Nevertheless: although the essays have failed, I continue to be convinced of the necessity to have written them and to have done it within the situation that we find ourselves. I continue to be convinced that for someone who suffered in his own skin the current rupture of the ground that supports us, the only dignified attitude to assume is that which seeks to regain the lost contact with concrete experience. And, afterward, to seek to articulate the unutterable. To seek to *mediate* the *immediate*.

What we are witnessing is the ultimate alienation of society as a whole. A collective madness, even in the psychiatric sense of the term. It is a madness followed by a galloping stupidity. Certainly: we cannot "overcome" such crazy stupidity: we are all, victims. But we can diagnose it, above all within ourselves. And this diagnosis demands a critical irony with regards to ourselves, a distancing from oneself that each one is obliged to effect by himself, in the solitude of a selfness that pierces the "self." I cannot see another method that could reconstitute a base for future human attitudes – whatever those may be – that could re-invert the vectors of significance of the codified world that is being established, and that could give meaning to the absurd that we are. First to the absurd itself, and after, through publishing, to contribute to give meaning to our-being-for-the Other. I cannot see another political attitude in this situation as it is "given" to us.

Post-history is rising. It is rising in two forms: in the stupidity of the programming apparatus, and in the form of the stupidity of the barbarian destroyers of apparatus. However, amidst this tide of ungoverned alienation, we continue to open for a concrete reality, which we experience today in the form of a solitude for death. Not only in the form of our own solitude for death, but through it, in the form of a solitude for the death of the Other. Despite the tide that surrounds us, and which swallows us, we are open for the recognition of ourselves within the Other. No longer, certainly, in society, but in the solitude of selfness. We are in this sense doubly negative, open for love, which *omnia vincit*. To be certain: we are programmed to be *Homines ludentes*. But this does not necessarily imply that we are programmed only to be robotized functionaries, objects. We may, equally, be players that play in function of the Other. Thus we may pass from being robots to once again being "the image of God," *through the back door*. To rupture the alienated symbolization and return to the concrete experience of our own death in the Other. To return, in sum, to being Human.

Univocal Publishing
123 North 3rd Street, #202
Minneapolis, MN 55401
www.univocalpublishing.com

ISBN 9781937561093
This work was composed in Berkely and Trajan.
All materials were printed and bound
in February 2013 at Univocal's atelier
in Minneapolis, USA.

The paper is Mohawk Via, Pure White Linen.
The letterpress cover was printed
on Crane's Lettra Pearl.
Both are archival quality and acid-free.

Flusser Archive Collection

Post-History

Natural: Mind

History Of the Devil

Doubt

Language and Reality

Foundational Concepts of Western Thought

Philosophy of Language

The Influence of Existential Thought Today